THE INSTANT MILLIONAIRE

Mark Fisher is a young Canadian millionaire with interests in property and publishing.

However success is not dependent on what you do in life, but how you do it. We can all achieve our personal and financial goals if we understand and practise the principles of success.

That is why this book was written, and it has now been published in more than a dozen languages as the tale of the Instant Millionaire has spread worldwide.

MARK FISHER

THE INSTANT MILLIONAIRE

A millionaire reveals how to achieve personal and financial success

HAMMOND

HAMMOND

The Instant Millionaire

© Mark Fisher 1988
Represented by The Cathy Miller Foreign Rights Agency, London

Previously published in Great Britain in 1988 and 1990
This edition published in 1993 and reprinted in 1994 by
Hammond Books
427 Great West Road, Hounslow, TW5 OBY

ISBN 1-898520-01-1

A CIP catalogue record for this book is available
from the British Library

Cover design by Carol Evans
Cover design © Hammond Books 1993
Typeset by Saxon Graphics Ltd, Derby
Printed and bound in Great Britain by
Biddles Ltd, Guildford and Kings Lynn

Distributed in Malaysia, Singapore and Brunei by
Crescent News (KL) SDN. BHD.,
P.O. Box 12333, 50774 Kuala Lumpur

'Every day, in every way,
I am getting better and better'

Émile Coué,
FRENCH PHYSICIAN

CONTENTS

THE
INSTANT
MILLIONAIRE

CHAPTER 1

*In which the young man consults a
wealthy relative*

T HERE was once a bright young man who wanted to get rich. He had had his fair share of disap-
pointments and setbacks, it couldn't be denied, and
yet he still believed in his lucky star.

While he waited for fortune to smile, he worked as
an assistant to an account executive in a second-league
advertising agency. He was inadequately paid and for
some time had felt that this job offered him little sat-
isfaction. His heart was simply no longer in it.

He dreamed of doing something else, perhaps of
writing a novel that would make him wealthy and
famous, ending his financial problems once and for
all. But wasn't his ambition a bit unrealistic? Did he
really have enough technique and talent to write a
bestseller or would the blank pages be filled with the
bleak ramblings of his inner misery?

His job had actually been a daily nightmare for
over a year now. He could barely stand his boss, who
spent most of each morning reading the newspaper
and writing memos before disappearing to indulge in

yet another three-hour lunch. His boss had also fine-tuned the art of changing his mind and giving contradictory orders, which didn't help matters.

Perhaps if it had only been his boss... but unfortunately, he was surrounded by colleagues who were also fed up with what they were doing. They seemed to have abandoned any sense of vision, to have given up altogether. He didn't dare tell any of them about his fantasy of dropping everything and becoming a writer. He knew they would only treat it as a joke. He was as cut off from the world as if he had been in a foreign country, unable to speak the language.

Every Monday morning he wondered how on earth he was going to survive another week at the office. He felt totally alienated from the files piled high on his desk, from the needs of clients clamouring to sell their cigarettes, their cars, their beer....

He had written a letter of resignation six months earlier, and had walked into his boss's office a dozen times with the letter burning in his pocket, but had never been quite able to go through with it. Funny, he would not have hesitated three or four years back. But now he seemed unsure of what to do. Something was holding him back, some kind of force, or was it simply cowardice? He seemed to have lost the nerve which had always got him what he wanted in the past.

Perhaps the fact that he had hung about waiting till the time was ripe, trying to find excuses for not jumping into action, wondering if he could indeed succeed, had turned him into a perpetual dreamer....

Did his paralysis spring from the fact that he was riddled with debts? Or was it because he had simply started to get old (a process which is inevitably triggered the minute you give up your vision of the future)?

To tell the truth, he had no idea what the problem was. And then, one day, when he was feeling especially frustrated, he suddenly thought of an uncle of his who happened to be a millionaire. His uncle might just be able to give him some advice, or better still, some money.

Known as a warm, friendly person, his uncle immediately agreed to see him, but refused to lend him any money, alleging that he wouldn't be doing him a favour.

'How old are you?' he asked, after listening to his tale of woe.

'Thirty-two,' the young man whispered timidly, knowing full well that his uncle's question was loaded with reproach.

'Do you know that by the time John Paul Getty was twenty-three he'd already made his first million? And that when I was your age, I had half a million. So how in the world is it that you are forced to borrow money at your age?'

'Beats me. I work like a dog, sometimes over fifty hours a week....'

'Do you really believe that hard work is what makes people rich?'

'I-I guess so... anyway, that's what I've always been led to believe.'

'How much do you make a year... £15,000?'

'Yeah, about that much,' replied the young man.

'Do you think that someone who earns £150,000 works ten times as many hours a week as you do? Obviously not! It would be physically impossible – there simply aren't more than 168 hours in a week. So if this person earns ten times more than you do without working any more than you do, then he must be doing something quite different from you. He must have a secret you are totally unaware of.'

'That's got to be it.'

'You're lucky you understand that at least. Most people don't even get that far. They're far too busy trying to earn a living to stop and think about how they could get rid of their money problems. Most people don't even spend an hour of their time trying to figure out how they could get rich and why they've never managed to do so.'

The young man had to admit that, despite his burning ambition and his dream of making a fortune, he, too, had never taken the time to really think his situation through. Everything seemed to distract him, preventing him from facing up to this task which was evidently of fundamental importance.

The young man's uncle grew silent for a while, then looked his nephew straight in the eye, his lips breaking into a gentle, though ironical, smile. 'Listen, I've decided to help you. I'm going to send you to the man who helped me get rich. He's called the Instant Millionaire. Perhaps you've heard of him.'

'No, never,' the young man replied.

'He chose this name himself because he claims that he became a millionaire overnight after discovering the true secret of making a fortune. He claims that he can help anyone become a millionaire overnight – or at least acquire the mentality of a millionaire. But tell me – do you really want to get rich?'

'More than anything in the world.'

'That's the first prerequisite. The major one. But it's not enough. You also have to know how.'

The young man shrugged his shoulders slightly, appearing to agree.

His uncle turned to a large map on the wall and pointed to a small, somewhat isolated town.

'That's where he lives. Have you ever been there?'

'No.'

'Why not give it a try? Go and find him. He just might reveal his secret to you. He lives in a fantastic house – the most beautiful one in the whole town. You shouldn't have any problem finding it.'

'Why don't you just tell me the secret right here and now? Then I won't have to take the trouble of going there.'

'Simply because I don't have the right to. When the Instant Millionaire confided it to me, the first thing he did was to make me swear never to tell it to anybody. However, he did say that I could tell anybody where I got it from.'

All of this seemed both surprising and involved to the young man. But it had aroused his curiosity.

'Are you sure you can't tell me anything?'

'Absolutely positive. What I can do is recommend you highly to the Instant Millionaire.'

Without further ado, his uncle pulled out a sheet of elegant writing paper from a drawer in a massive oak desk, took his pen and hastily scribbled a few lines on it. He then folded the letter, sealed it in an envelope and, with a smile on his face, handed it to his nephew.

'Here's your introduction.' he said. 'And here's the millionaire's address. One last thing. You must promise not to read this letter. If you do read it, it probably won't be any more use to you.... But if ever you do open it, despite my warning, and you still want it to work for you, you'll have to pretend that you haven't opened it. But how can you undo what's already been done?'

The young man didn't have the vaguest idea what his uncle was talking about, but let it go at that. His uncle had always had the reputation of being eccentric. And after all, the man was doing him a favour... so he decided not to press the point. He thanked his uncle and left.

CHAPTER 2

In which the young man meets an elderly gardener

THAT same afternoon he sped off towards the Instant Millionaire's town. How hard was it going to be to get to meet the Instant Millionaire? Was he going to welcome his unannounced visitor and reveal his secret method of getting rich?

Just before arriving at the millionaire's house the young man was overcome by curiosity and, despite his uncle's words of warning, opened the letter of introduction that his uncle had so kindly written for him. Flabbergasted, he wondered whether a mistake had been made or whether his uncle had wanted to play a joke on him – the "letter" was only a blank sheet of paper!

Disgusted, he was about to get rid of it, but he was now in sight of the millionaire's house and noticed a security guard, who surely would have seen him throw it away. True to type, his face bore a stony expression without the slightest hint of a smile. In fact, it looked as impenetrable as the enclosed "fortress" he was aiming to protect.

'What can I do for you?' the guard asked drily.

'I'd like to meet the Instant Millionaire....'

'Do you have an appointment?'

'No, but....'

'Well then, do you have a letter of introduction?' the guard enquired.

Of course he had one, but there was nothing written on it! It didn't take the young man long to think of a trick that might get him out of this situation. He pulled the letter halfway out of his pocket and quickly stuffed it back again. This didn't satisfy the guard, however.

'May I see your letter?'

The young man was now stuck. he thought, 'If I give him the letter, he'll think I'm trying to pull a fast one on him. But if I don't, he won't let me in.'

He was faced with a seemingly insurmountable dilemma.

Then he remembered his uncle's words of advice, which he hadn't understood at the time. 'If you open the letter, you must pretend that you haven't.'

Wasn't that the only thing left to do? He handed the letter to the guard who read it, so to speak. His face remained totally expressionless.

'Fine,' he said, giving it back to the young man.

'You may come in.'

The guard then led him to the front door of the millionaire's luxurious, Tudor-style home. An impeccably dressed butler opened the door.

'What do you want?' he asked.

'To meet the Instant Millionaire.'

'He's busy, and unable to see you just at the moment. Please wait for him in the garden.'

The butler then accompanied the young man to the entrance of a garden that looked more like a park. In the middle of it stood a pond. The young man wandered in a little way, admiring the beautiful trees. Then he caught sight of a gardener who looked at least seventy. He was bent over a rose bush that he was trimming, and a wide-brimmed straw hat concealed his eyes. When the young man approached him, the gardener broke off his work to welcome him. He smiled. He had bright, cheerful blue eyes that looked as ageless as the sun.

'What have you come here for?' he asked in a warm and friendly voice.

'I've come to meet the Instant Millionaire.'

'Oh, I see. And for what reason, if you don't mind my asking?'

'Well, I... I'd simply like to ask him for advice....'

'Obviously....'

The gardener was just about to go back to his roses when he thought better of it and asked the young man: 'Oh, by the way, you wouldn't have a fiver on you, would you?'

'A fiver?' exclaimed the young man, blushing. 'It's just that... that's all I've got on me, £5.'

'Perfect. That's all I need.'

Even though he appeared to be begging, the gardener still looked very dignified. His manner exuded exceptional grace and charm.

'I'd really like to give it to you,' replied the young man, 'but the only problem is that I wouldn't have any money left to get home.'

'Are you planning to go home today?'

'No-o-o.... I mean, I've no idea,' said the young man, now quite confused. 'I don't want to leave until I have seen the Instant Millionaire.'

'But if you don't need this money today, why are you so reluctant to lend it to me? You might not need it tomorrow. Who knows...? You might be a millionaire .'

This reasoning didn't sound completely logical to the young man, but he lacked the strength to put up any further arguments. So when the gardener repeated his request, he handed the money over to him. The gardener's face broke into a smile.

'Most people are afraid of asking for things, and when they finally do they don't insist enough. That's a mistake.'

At that moment the butler arrived in the garden and spoke to the old man in a very respectful tone of voice: 'Sir, could you please let me have £5? The cook's leaving today and insists on being paid the money we owe him. I'm just £5 short.'

The gardener smiled. He stuck his hand into his pocket and pulled out a thick wad of notes. He must have had thousands of pounds, what with the £20 and

£50 notes the young man caught sight of. The gardener peeled off the £5 note that the young man had
reluctantly agreed to give him and handed it to the
butler, who thanked him, bowed somewhat obse-
quiously and quickly disappeared into the house.

The young man was outraged. How did the gardener have the gall to confiscate the last £5 he had in
the world when his pockets were stuffed with money?

'Why did you ask me for £5?' he muttered, trying
as hard as he could to conceal the boiling rage he felt.
'You didn't need it!'

'But of course I did. Look, I don't have any £5
notes,' he explained, thumbing through the fat roll of
banknotes. 'You surely don't think I was going to give
him a £50 note, do you?'

'Why on earth do you keep so much money on
you?'

'It's my pocket money,' replied the gardener. 'I
always keep £10,000 on me in case of an emergency.'

'£10,000?' spluttered the young man, aghast.

Suddenly everything became clear – the super-
polite butler, that incredible amount of pocket
money....

'You're the Instant Millionaire, aren't you?'

'For the time being,' replied the gardener. 'I'm
glad you've come. But tell me, who sent you?'

'My uncle, he said he was the first person with
whom you shared the secret.'

'Oh yes. I remember him. He came to see me
many years ago. He was a very original thinker – like

all self-made men, in fact. But tell me, how is it that you yourself aren't rich yet? Have you ever seriously asked yourself that question?'

'Not really.'

'That's perhaps the first thing you should do. If you want, think aloud in front of me. I'll try to follow your line of reasoning.'

The young man made a few feeble attempts and then gave up.

'I see,' said the millionaire. 'You're not used to thinking out loud. Do you know that there are lots of young people of your age who are already rich? Some of them are even millionaires. Others are just on the verge of getting their first million. And did you know that, when he was twenty-six, Aristotle Onassis already had £350,000 in the bank when he left South America for England, where he was dreaming of setting up his shipping Empire?'

'Only twenty-six?' asked the young man.

'That's right. And when he started out he had only £250 to his name. He didn't have a university degree or skills – and he certainly didn't have any contacts....'

'But now it's time for dinner,' the old man observed. 'Would you like to join me?'

'Thank you very much. I'd love to.'

The young man followed the Instant Millionaire who, despite his age, still had a lively bounce to his step. They made their way into the dining room where the table had already been set for two.

'Please sit down,' invited the Instant Millionaire.

He pointed to the end of the table, the place usually reserved for the host. He himself sat to the right of his young guest, directly in front of a beautiful hourglass engraved with the trite motto: TIME IS MONEY. The butler arrived with a bottle of wine and filled their glasses.

'Let's have a drink to your first million,' said the millionaire, raising his glass.

He took a sip, the only one he had all evening. He also ate very frugally – just a few mouthfuls from a delicious salmon steak.

'Do you like what you do for a living?' the millionaire asked the young man.

'I suppose so.'

'Make sure you're positive about that. All the millionaires I've known – and I've met quite a few over the years – loved their occupations. For them, working became almost a leisure activity, as agreeable as a hobby. That's why most of the rich rarely take holidays.Why should they deprive themselves of what they like so much? That would be sheer self-punishment. And that's also why they continue working even after becoming millionaires several times over.... Incidentally, although enjoying your work is an absolute must, it's not enough. To get rich, you have to know the secret. Tell me, do you at least believe this secret exists?'

'Yes, I do.'

'Good. That's the first step. Most people don't believe in it. Besides, they don't even believe they can become rich. And they're right. Anybody who doesn't think he can grow rich rarely does. You have to start by believing that you can, and then crave it passionately. But I should add that many people – the majority, in fact – aren't ready to accept this secret, even if it's revealed to them in very simple terms. In fact, their greatest limitation is their own lack of imagination. That's basically why the true secret of wealth is the best-kept secret in the world.

'It's a little like the purloined letter in Edgar Allan Poe's story,' the Instant Millionaire went on. 'Do you remember it? It's the one about the letter the police were searching for in someone's house and could never find because, instead of being hidden away somewhere, it was lying in the least likely spot – in plain sight! That story is a clever illustration of one of Emerson's principles. What prevented the police from finding the letter was their lack of imagination, or, if you prefer, their built-in prejudices. They weren't expecting to find it there – so they never got their hands on it.'

The young man was listening to the millionaire with rapt attention. No one had ever spoken to him like this before, and his curiosity was deeply aroused. He was burning to find out what the secret was. In any case, one thing was sure: even if the millionaire didn't really have the secret, he was certainly a genius in the art of setting the scene. Most of all, he knew how to explain things simply and clearly, unless it was only a skilfully contrived illusion.

CHAPTER 3

In which the young man learns to seize opportunities and take risks

'NOW, after all you've heard, how much money are you willing to pay to get the secret of wealth?'

The millionaire's question took the young man by surprise. 'Even if I *were* willing to spend money to get it, I haven't got a penny. So that's a hard question to answer.'

'But *if* you had money, how much would you be willing to pay?' The millionaire then quickly added: 'Name a figure, any figure. The first one that comes to mind.'

The young man couldn't possibly evade the question now. The millionaire was asking for a specific answer and he couldn't let his host down.

'I don't know,' he replied. '£100...?'

The millionaire burst out laughing, the first time the young man had heard him do so. It was a very individual kind of laugh, clear and crystalline.

'Only £100? You don't really believe it exists, do you? If you did, you'd surely be ready to pay a lot more for it. Come on – I'll give you a second chance. Name another figure – this isn't a game, but a very serious matter.'

The young man started thinking it over. He'd do anything in the world not to make the millionaire laugh again. But he didn't want to name a figure that would compromise himself, either.

'I don't mind playing your little game,' he said. 'But remember, I'm flat broke.'

'Don't worry about that.'

'But if I don't have any money, my hands are tied,' countered the young man, somewhat bewildered.

'Oh, my!' exclaimed the millionaire. 'We've got a long way to go! Since time eternal, the rich have been using other people's money to amass their fortunes. Anyone really serious has never needed money to make money. By that I mean personal cash. Besides, you must have a cheque book on you....'

The young man would have liked to deny it. However, ironically enough, that very morning he had stuffed his cheque book into his pocket. God knows why, since he had exactly £12.28 in his account – certainly not enough to paint the town red! The young man wouldn't have thought twice about lying, but the millionaire had such a piercing gaze, apparently capable of scrutinising the tiniest recesses of his mind. Almost as if he were confessing a deep, dark secret the young man heard himself stutter: 'Yes, I br-brought it with me.'

At that moment, he found himself pulling his cheque book out as automatically as a robot obeying its master's orders, even though an urge to rebel momentarily crossed his mind. He felt spellbound by this man, like someone in the hands of a hypnotist. Yet he wasn't afraid of the millionaire, who radiated goodwill – even though his manner was somewhat ironical.

'Fine,' replied the millionaire. '*Now* can you see there's no problem?'

He uncapped an elegant pen and handed it to the young man.

'Write it out for the amount you have in mind and sign the cheque.'

'But I don't know how much to write.'

'All right. Put down, say... £10,000.'

The millionaire uttered this figure in a perfectly straightforward way, without a shred of arrogance. The young man almost jumped out of his skin. There were no two ways about it: the millionaire was poking fun at him... unless he was simply a brilliant con man!

'£10,000!!' exclaimed the young man. 'You've got to be joking.'

'Put down £20,000 if you like,' replied the millionaire, so calmly that the young man no longer knew whether he spoke seriously or in jest.

'Even £10,000 seems far too much. Anyway, you couldn't cash the cheque because it would bounce. And all I'd get out of it would be an angry bank manager wondering whether I'd gone mad or something. And he'd be right!'

'That's exactly how I undertook my biggest deal ever. I signed a cheque for £100,000 and then had to scramble around to find the money to cover it. But if I hadn't made out that cheque right then and there, I'd have missed an excellent opportunity.

'That was one of my first major business lessons,' he continued. 'People who waste time waiting for all the perfect conditions to fall into place never get anything done. The ideal time for action is NOW! And another lesson this little anecdote can teach you is this: if you want to succeed in life, you have to make sure you have no choice in the matter. You have to put your back to the wall. People who shilly-shally and refuse to take risks on the pretext that they don't have all the elements in hand never get anywhere. The reason is simple. When you cut off all your exits and put your back to the wall, you mobilise all your inner powers. At this point you want something to happen with every fibre of your being. So why hesitate now, young man? Put your back to the wall. Make out that £10,000 cheque to me.'

The young man wrote out the cheque, slowly filling in first the figures, then the words. But when he came to sign it, he simply couldn't do it.

'I've never written out a cheque as large as this in my life.'

'If you want to become a millionaire, you'll have to start some day. You have to get used to signing cheques much larger than this one. This is only the beginning.'

Even so, the young man still couldn't sign it right away. Everything was happening so quickly. He was about to hand over a cheque for £10,000 to a man he'd just met for the very first time and who was promising a pretty dubious secret in exchange.

'What's stopping you from signing it?' asked the millionaire. 'Everything's relative under the sun. In no time at all, this amount will appear insignificant to you.'

'It's not the amount,' mumbled the young man, who by this time scarcely knew what he was saying.

'Well, what is it then?'

He was just about to answer when the millionaire cut him off. 'I know why you can't sign it. You don't really believe my secret will turn you into a millionaire. If you were absolutely convinced, you'd sign in a flash.'

To be sure of convincing him, or rather, to illustrate his point more clearly, the millionaire added: 'If you were really and truly positive that this secret would help you earn £50,000 in less than a year, without your having to work harder than you do now – and even by working less – would you sign this cheque?'

'I'm quite sure I would,' he was forced to agree. 'I'd make a £40,000 profit.'

'So sign it. I formally guarantee that you'll be able to earn this amount.'

'Would you be willing to put that down in writing?'

Once again the millionaire burst out laughing. 'I like you, young man. You're determined to cover your back. That's often a very prudent thing to do. Even if you're absolutely sure about your resources, it doesn't mean that you should trust the first person who comes your way.'

He then stood up, rummaged about in a drawer and pulled out a ready-made formula that he must have already used under similar circumstances. This didn't go down very well with the young man. Was the old man mass-producing his secret and selling it to every Tom, Dick and Harry who showed up?

The millionaire wrote out the guarantee and handed it to the young man, who skimmed over it quickly and seemed satisfied with what he'd read. Then the old man suddenly changed his mind.

'I've got another idea,' he said. 'How about a bet?'

He took a coin from his pocket and bounced it up and down in the palm of his hand.

'Let's play heads or tails. If I lose, I'll give you the £10,000 cash I have in my pocket. If I win, you give me the cheque. In either case, let's forget about the guarantee.'

The young man took a minute to think over this highly unusual proposition. It wasn't a bad idea. In fact, it was so appealing that it made him wonder why the devil the old man was suggesting it in the first place. It looked too good to be honest.

'The only problem,' he said, 'is what I told you. I've only got small change in the bank. Even if I give you this cheque, you won't be able to cash it.'

'No problem,' said the millionaire. 'I'm in no hurry. I'll even wait until the next time I see you. Why not postdate it a year to the day from now?'

'All right. Under those conditions I accept the bet.'

He had now worked out that in any event he had a full year to change banks, close his account or simply stop the cheque. He should have thought of that before. He had nothing to lose. And with the millionaire's new offer he could even earn £10,000 in a few seconds flat, without having to do an ounce of work!

In spite of himself, a self-satisfied smile flitted across his lips. Guiltily, he hoped the millionaire had not noticed it, but then he was a pretty sharp character. Hard to say. At that very moment the millionaire proposed a minor clarification, which immediately confirmed the young man's doubts.

'There's just one thing. In case you do lose the bet, I'd like you to swear solemnly that you'll honour this cheque.'

The young man blushed. This old man's wilier than a fox, he thought. The millionaire seemed to read his mind like an open book. The young man gave him his word, but just as the millionaire was about to toss the coin he abruptly interrupted him.

'May I see the coin?' said the young man.

The millionaire smiled. 'No doubt about it. I really like you, young man. You're cautious. That'll help you avoid a lot of mistakes. But make sure it doesn't cause you to miss out on a lot of good opportunities.'

The millionaire then graciously handed over the coin. As soon as the young man had carefully examined both sides, the millionaire asked him to call.

'Tails,' he replied.

The Instant Millionaire tossed the coin. The young man's heart began to beat as wildly as if he were on his first date! This was the first time he'd ever had the chance of winning £10,000 - not an amount to sneeze at! As he watched the coin spinning in the air, his anxiety mounted sharply. It rolled on to the table, and finally stood still.

'Heads!' decreed the millionaire gleefully, nevertheless quickly adding a sympathetic: 'Sorry.'

It was hard to say whether he was being sincere or merely polite.

The young man then resolved to sign the cheque. He couldn't help trembling a little, even so. He would probably get used to signing big cheques like this one day, but at this point it made him feel very strange indeed. He gave the cheque to the millionaire, who examined it briefly, folded it and put it in his pocket.

'Now,' said the young man, 'can I have the secret?'

'But of course,' retorted the millionaire. 'Do you have some paper on you? I'll write it down for you. That way, you won't forget it.'

The young man had a hard time grasping his words. The millionaire surely couldn't expect a single sheet of paper to hold the entire secret – especially a secret he'd just bought for £10,000!

'Sorry. I don't have any paper on me.'

The millionaire made his heart do somersaults again, asking him: 'But didn't you have a letter of introduction when you arrived here? The people your uncle sent me over the years always had a letter.'

The young man still had the letter on him. He took it out of his pocket, thinking that the old man certainly didn't miss a trick.

He handed it over, carefully watching the man's face as he opened it. But the millionaire didn't seem at all surprised to find it was completely blank. He took his pen, leaned over the table and was about to write something when he raised his head and asked the young man to go and fetch the butler.

'You'll find him in the kitchen, at the far end of that corridor over there,' explained the millionaire.

As the young man came back with the butler, the millionaire was sealing the envelope. He was smiling, and seemed pleased with himself.

'Our young guest will be spending the night,' he said to the butler. 'Would you take him to his room, please?' Then, turning to the young man, he said, 'Here's the secret.' The millionaire stood up and handed over the envelope, solemnly shaking his hand as if he had just wrapped up one of the most important deals he had ever made in his life.

'The only thing I must ask you to do is to wait until you're alone in your room before opening the envelope and reading the secret.... Oh, there's one more condition. Before you may read what I've written, you have to promise to spend part of your life sharing this secret with those less fortunate than you. If you agree, you'll be the last person to whom I'll ever give the secret directly. My work will be over. Then I'll be able to take care of my roses in a much larger garden.

'If you don't feel ready to share this secret,' he ended, 'you still have time to back out. But then of course you won't be able to open the envelope. I'll give you back your cheque. And you'll be free to go home and get on with the same life you've been leading up to now.'

Now that he finally had his hands on the letter containing the famous secret, there was no way the young man was going to back out. His curiosity had got the better of him.

'I promise,' he replied.

CHAPTER 4

In which the young man finds himself a prisoner

SOON he was all alone in his room, which was so luxurious that he couldn't help examining it from top to bottom. He seemed to have forgotten the precious letter that he had paid so dearly for. He went up to the only window in the room, which was very high off the ground and looked out onto the park. He could even see the garden where he had first spotted the millionaire looking after his roses with such tender, loving care.

Night had fallen, but a full moon cast a luminescent glow over everything. The young man was now brimming over with impatience. He was finally going to discover the secret to making a fortune that had eluded him for so many years.

He opened the envelope, unfolded the letter and began to peruse it. Or that's what he would like to have done if the sheet of paper staring him in the face had not been completely blank! He turned it over. There wasn't the tiniest squiggle on either side! He'd been fool enough to let the old man swindle him.

He'd handed over a cheque for a mind-boggling sum in exchange for a secret that didn't exist!

And yet the millionaire had seemed nice enough in the end. He'd even started feeling fond of the old man, who looked honest enough. The young man realised he should have been more careful, that there was some truth after all in the saying that totally honest people never get rich.

He was forced to admit that he had no business sense at all – probably the very reason he'd fallen for the old man's trick!

A feeling of rebellion engulfed him, and in a fit of rage he ripped the letter in two and dropped it on to the thick, plush carpet. His only consolation was that ridicule couldn't kill anyone – otherwise his life would now be worthless.

What could he do? There was something unreal about this whole affair. He'd let himself be lured into a well-sprung trap. He had one alternative: to escape as quickly as possible. Who knows? Maybe his life was in danger, too. He had to decide fast. He didn't want to spend the night in this place.

The best way would be to sneak out as quietly as possible. He tiptoed to the door and slowly turned the handle. Damn! The door was bolted from the outside. He was a prisoner. The window was the only other exit. He ran to it. It slid open easily, but the problem was that it stood about thirty feet above the ground. If he jumped, he'd surely break his neck. Better think of another escape route. His one and only hope was to ring for the butler. What else could he do? Vanishing silently into the night was now out of the question.

He pulled the bell and waited. No one came. He rang again. Nothing.

Total silence filled the house. Everybody must be asleep. Maybe the bell was out of order. In that case, the only thing left was to shout. But he couldn't do it. What if the millionaire were acting in good faith, despite all appearances to the contrary? The young man would look like a fool, waking everybody up in the middle of the night.

Finally he decided to get some sleep. However, that was no easy matter. The events of that day raced before his eyes. In spite of all the arguments he raised, there was little he could do to fight off the feeling of absurdity that was beginning to overwhelm him. The blank sheet of paper he had bought for £10,000 kept drifting before his eyes as if bent on mocking him. Fortunately, sleep rescued him from this waking nightmare. But not for long. He began dreaming of a stranger urging him repeatedly to sign a thick document of the utmost importance as if his life depended on it. He protested vehemently. There must be some mistake – the document was totally blank....

CHAPTER 5

In which the young man learns to have faith

THE next morning, the young man felt as if he'd been run over by a three-ton lorry. Ironically, the breeze wafting in through the open window had gently lifted the infamous letter and magically reassembled the pieces at the foot of his bed. It was the first thing he laid eyes on that morning, and a fit of rage swept over him. He had slept in his clothes: now they were all wrinkled, but he couldn't care less. He had one thought in mind: to find the old man, give him back his secret and get the cheque back. The young man glanced at himself in the mirror just long enough to notice that he looked pretty awful. This only bolstered his determination.

He ran his fingers through his hair a couple of times and headed towards the door, instantly recalling that it had been locked the night before and that he was perhaps still a prisoner. But he wasn't. He strode angrily out, heading for the dining room.

He found the Instant Millionaire calmly sitting at the table, dressed in the same clothes he'd had on the day before: a gardener's outfit which was modest and clean but surprisingly threadbare. His large, pointed, wide-brimmed hat, which could have looked like a sorcerer's had it not been made of straw, was lying in front of him on the table. The millionaire was tossing a coin and counting. He had got up to eight.

'Nine,' he muttered without taking his eyes off the coin. 'Ten.' But he didn't make it to eleven, muttering 'Damn.' He lifted his head while retrieving the coin. 'I've never been able to go beyond ten,' he remarked. 'I get tails ten times in a row and then invariably heads on the eleventh throw, even though I throw it the same way each time.'

A thought suddenly flashed through the young man's mind. He realised then and there that he had been duped a second time the night before. There was no way he could have won his bet with either heads or tails.

'My father, who was a magician, would regularly get to fifteen,' explained the millionaire. 'I didn't inherit his talent.'

The young man asked to see the coin. After the millionaire had cheerfully given it to him, he threw it onto the table.

Heads. Tails. Heads. Tails. It obviously wasn't a trick coin, unless there was some secret mechanism that had escaped his notice.

'There was nothing dishonest about our bet yesterday,' admitted the millionaire. 'I simply displayed my skill at handling money. Besides, it's not the first time people have come to the same conclusion. They take skilfullness for dishonesty.'

The young man didn't know how to reply to that. Then he remembered why he had come down to see the man. He brandished the letter in the air and threw it on the table.

'You did a fine job of tricking me, sir. You made yourself some easy money there – £10,000 for a blank sheet of paper.'

'It's not blank. It's the secret of wealth,' the millionaire corrected him.

The young man was waiting for the millionaire to apologise for this regrettable misunderstanding. 'Well, you're going to have to explain yourself. Do you take me for an idiot?'

'An idiot? Of course not. You're simply lacking in perspicacity. It's quite normal. Your mind is still young and immature.'

'Maybe it is, but I can certainly recognise a blank piece of paper when I see one - and the fact that you've pulled a fast one on me.'

'I don't see what more you can want. I assure you that you can become very rich indeed with just this blank piece of paper. That's all I needed to become an instant millionaire way back when.... But since my time is short and I must soon go back to tend my beloved roses, I'll help you. Listen carefully, because as soon as you apply this secret successfully, you'll have to explain it to others. Once you've freed yourself of the shackles of poverty, you'll have to show the way to those still bound hand and foot. May I ask you to repeat the promise you made yesterday?'

There was no doubt about it – the millionaire was the most extraordinarily persuasive man he'd ever met in his life! Barely a few minutes ago the young man had been ready to curse him with all the volubility possessed only by the young, and now he was almost eating out of the old man's palm!

The idea of refusing the millionaire didn't even cross his mind. He made his solemn oath again. The millionaire's face broke out into a smile, a smile as strange as the one that had darted across his lips the previous day when the young man had first met him.

'I've decided to tell you the secret, since you haven't been able to discover it on your own. I must warn you again that it'll probably seem too easy to be true. But don't let its simplicity deceive you. Each time you begin to have doubts, remember Mozart. True genius resides in simplicity. Since you're still young, you'll tend to have doubts in the beginning. With time, as wealth is magnetically attracted to you in a most unexpected way, you'll begin to understand.'

'I'll be honest with you,' said the young man. 'That's exactly what I've been hoping for with all my heart: to understand!'

'So much the better. Faith quickly follows true understanding. Once you've grasped the secret, you'll know why you believe in it. But in the beginning, despite its simplicity, this secret will seem so surprising that you'll be incapable of understanding it – or even believing it, for that matter. So I'm asking you to make a small act of faith. It's a little like a sceptic trying to relate to God. If God exists, you'll have gained everything because of your faith. If He doesn't, you won't have lost a thing. The same goes for this secret.'

CHAPTER 6

In which the young man learns to focus on a goal

'FEEL free to ask me any questions that cross your mind,' said the millionaire. 'It'll be a pleasure for me to answer them. Soon you won't be able to do so, and since our time together is limited let's not waste it in futile discussions. Here's a pen. Do you have the piece of paper?'

'Here it is.'

'Do you really want to become rich?'

'I most certainly do.'

'All right, then. Write down the amount of money you want and how much time you'll allow yourself to make it in. This is the mysterious secret of wealth.'

The young man thought that the Instant Millionaire was pulling his leg again. 'Do you think money's going to drop like pennies from Heaven just because I write a couple of numbers down on paper?'

'Yes, I do,' was all the millionaire saw fit to say. 'Your reaction doesn't surprise me in the least. I warned you that the secret would be simple, and yet, you're still dumbfounded.... Allow me to add one point before I attempt to make things clearer. All the millionaires I've met confessed to me that they became rich the moment they set themselves an amount and a deadline by which to acquire it.'

'I'm sorry, but I still don't understand. What good does it do me to write down a figure and a deadline?'

'If you don't know where you're heading, the chances are you'll never get anywhere.'

'Maybe, but that seems to smack of magic to me.'

'But that's exactly what it is – the secret magic of a quantified objective. Let's look at the problem from a different angle. Suppose you're trying to get a job. You go through all the necessary steps and finally land an interview. A short while later, you're told that you've been short-listed. Then you find out that the job is yours and that you'll be making a lot of money. How would you react? For a start, you'd be really pleased with yourself. Being chosen from dozens, perhaps hundreds, of candidates – what a feat! And since jobs are rather scarce and you were unemployed for three months, or perhaps you already had a job, but had outgrown it over a year ago, you'd think this was a very lucky break indeed. But once your initial euphoria had passed, what would be your next reaction?'

'Well, I'd wonder when the job would start. Then, I'd like to know the exact meaning of "a lot of money". All things being relative in this world, I'd try and find out exactly how much the salary was going to be and what kind of benefits would be offered.'

'You've taken the words right out of my mouth. If, for example, you asked your new boss what he meant by "a lot of money" and all he did was guarantee that you were definitely going to earn a lot, you wouldn't be any further ahead, would you? Worse still, you'd probably start having second thoughts about his honesty. The fact that he was refusing to name a specific figure would quite possibly mean that there was something shady going on or that your salary wasn't going to be as generous as he'd been implying. Similarly, if he refused to tell you the exact date you were supposed to start the job, you wouldn't be very happy about it, would you? You'd try to pin him down.'

'I suppose I would,' agreed the young man, finding no fault with the old man's straightforward arguments.

'And despite insisting on it, if you still couldn't get the details you wanted then you might just prefer to turn it down and start looking elsewhere. In fact, you'd be fully justified in doing so.'

'Right you are. The employer would be either stringing me a line or an out-and-out crook. I'd have to admit that, either way, this job offer left a lot to be desired.'

The millionaire looked as content as Socrates must have felt after a particularly arduous question-and-answer session with his pupils. He paused a moment before proceeding, his lips still set in the same teasing but basically good natured smile: 'A little while ago, the questions you asked your imaginary employer were aimed at getting hard facts. Right? Just knowing that you were going to earn a lot of money wasn't enough. You also wanted to know how much. Finding out that you'd got the job didn't satisfy you, either. You also wanted to know the exact starting date. In addition, you'd probably want all of this down in writing because a contract adds backbone to a verbal agreement. Of course, a person's word should be enough. But words are ephemeral, the written word permanent. The same goes for life. What most people, or at least the unsuccessful ones, are unaware of is that life gives us exactly what we ask from it. The first thing to do, however, is to ask for exactly what we want. If your request is vague, whatever you get will be just as muddled. If you ask for the minimum, you'll get the minimum. And don't be surprised if that's all you get. After all, that's what you asked for.'

The millionaire made sure the young man was following what he was saying before continuing: 'Any request you make must be formulated in the same way. Above all it must be absolutely precise. As far as wealth is concerned, we must establish an amount and a deadline by which to make it. What do people generally do? Even those who want money and lots of it all make the same mistake. If you need convincing, just ask someone exactly how much money he wants to earn next year. Ask him to reply right off the cuff. If this person is really on the road to success, if he really knows where he's going, and if he doesn't mind confiding in you, he should be able to answer immediately. However, nine people out of ten will be incapable of answering this simple question off the top of their head. That is the most common mistake. Life wants to know exactly what you expect from it. If you don't ask for anything, you won't get anything.

'Now let's do the same test with you,' the old man continued. 'You told me you'd like to get rich.'

'Definitely.'

'Now can you tell me how much you'd like to earn next year?'

The young man suddenly found himself at a loss for words. He had no trouble following the old man's line of reasoning. In fact he agreed with it wholeheartedly. And yet he had to admit that he belonged to the vast majority of people who want to get rich but don't know how much they really want to make. He was embarrassed and his face turned brick-red.

'I don't know,' he was forced to admit. 'I think I've just understood one of my mistakes – perhaps the most fundamental one.'

'It's indeed a serious mistake. Let's try to correct it. Come on. Write down the amount you have in mind.'

'I really don't have the vaguest idea,' muttered the young man.

'And yet it's so easy. Write down the amount you'd like to earn between now and next year. I know what we'll do. Take a few minutes to think it over. When the time's up, you've *got* to write down an amount. As for the deadline, we said one year from now. So all you have to think about is the amount. Get going – time's slipping away!'

As he said this, he picked up the golden hourglass on the table and turned it over.

The young man quickly got into the spirit of the game, if you could call it that, since this was the very first time he'd ever had to think so hard in all his life. All sorts of absurd numbers flitted about uncontrollably in his head. Time was running out. When the last grain of sand had fallen, he still hadn't settled on a specific figure.

'Good,' said the millionaire, who hadn't taken his eyes away from the hourglass for a minute. 'What figure do you have in mind?'

The young man wrote down the most attainable figure he could think of. His trembling fingers slowly traced the individual numbers.

'£30,000!' exclaimed the millionaire. 'That's pretty low – but it's a start anyway. I would have preferred £300,000. You've got quite a lot of work to do before becoming an instant millionaire. But you'll see. This job won't be as tiring as most people imagine it to be. Nevertheless it'll be the most important work you'll ever do in your life, no matter which occupation you end up choosing. It's called working on yourself.'

CHAPTER 7

In which the young man gets to know the value of self-image

THE butler came in, bringing coffee and croissants. The young man hadn't had breakfast and the emotional turmoil he had experienced the night before had whetted his appetite. He ate while the lesson continued. This is how it went:

'I'm going to ask you a series of questions,' said the Instant Millionaire, 'to help you understand what happened to you during your minute of reflection, which must have seemed quite short to you.'

'It certainly did.'

'The first observation you must make is that the amount you wrote down on that piece of paper means much more than you think it does. In fact, this amount represents almost to a penny what you think you're worth. In your eyes, whether you are willing to admit it or not, you're worth £30,000 a year. Not a penny more and not a penny less.'

'I don't see why you say that,' observed the young man. 'The fact that I chose that particular amount means I'm level-headed and have both feet firmly on the ground. I can't see how I can earn more for the time being. After all, I don't have a degree, I don't have a good job and my bank balance is virtually nil.'

'Your way of thinking is valid, no doubt – in any case, I respect it. The only problem is that this attitude is the cause of your current situation. External circumstances are not really very important. Keep this well in mind: all the events in your life, be they emotional, social or professional, are a mirror image of your thoughts. But since your mind is still unformed it can't take in this principle yet. Your mind continues to accept the rather widespread illusion that external factors play a part in determining your life, whereas in reality everything in life is basically a matter of attitude. Life is exactly how we picture it to be. Everything that happens to you is brought on by your thoughts. So if you want to change your life, you must start by changing your thoughts. No doubt you consider this a bit trite. Many "rational" individuals stubbornly refute this principle.'

Realising that the young man was hanging on to his every word, the millionaire quickly added: 'All those who have accomplished great things in life, regardless of the field, have always ignored the objections raised by rational thinkers and intellectuals. No matter what they say, their thinking is essentially materialistic. They argue and reason things out. But when it comes down to it, their discussions are pretty sterile.

'However,' he continued, 'you musn't believe that I'm against intelligence. Quite the contrary. Reasoning and logic are necessary in order to achieve success. But they aren't enough. They must be instruments and faithful servants, nothing more. Yet in most cases they become roadblocks in the way of great achievements, which are created only by those who have faith in the powers of the mind. These successful people never let circumstances bother them too much, and they attract wealth to themselves almost miraculously. When you come down to it, the circumstances facing great achievers in the past were no different from those facing their contemporaries. Often, indeed, circumstances were even more difficult, but this situation simply caused them to tap even deeper into their inner strength. All these achievers firmly believed that they could accomplish great things. All those who became rich were deeply convinced that they could get rich. And that's why they succeeded.

'But let's get back to our piece of paper,' he finished, 'and answer this question. That £30,000 figure you wrote down was surely not the first one that came to your mind, was it?'

'You're right. It wasn't.'

'What was it, then?'

'I can't really say. My head was crowded with so many figures.'

'For instance?'

'Well, £50,000.'

51

'And why didn't you write it down?'

'I don't know. I suppose it seemed totally out of reach.'

'It'll remain that way until you believe you can reach it. Since you started with only £30,000 we've got a big job ahead of us – otherwise you'll take a very long time to become a millionaire. So write down the highest figure that still appears achievable to you.'

The young man obeyed him. After a moment of reflection, he wrote down £40,000.

'Congratulations,' the Instant Millionaire responded quickly. 'You've just earned £10,000 in a few seconds. Not bad, eh?'

'But I haven't earned it yet.'

'It's as if you had. You've taken the biggest step. You expanded your self-image by considering that you could earn £40,000 instead of £30,000. It's not a major leap forward, but it's progress all the same. After all, Rome wasn't built in a day. Inside you lies an obscure city, a kind of Rome – as it does in every human being, by the way. Astonishingly enough, this city is exactly the way you picture it to be. It's surprisingly flexible. The size of your city depends on the exact circumference you give it. Few people know that this inner city exists. The boundaries you set up for it are commonly known as your "self-image". By increasing the figure you wrote down, you set into motion the process of expanding your city limits. Your inner Rome grew at the same time. Or at least it's beginning to grow. All wise thinkers have said for ages that the greatest limitation man can impose on himself, and thus the greatest obstacle to his success, is mental. Expand your mental limits and you will expand your life. Explode your limitations and you will explode the limitations of your life. The conditions in your life will change as if by magic. This I solemnly swear to you.'

'But how can I find out what my mental limitations are?' the young man asked. 'All this seems plausible to me, yet at the same time quite abstract.'

'I've just finished explaining how to find the boundary that encloses your mind and corresponds to your self-image,' said the millionaire. 'You translated it into concrete terms when you wrote down that figure. It's fascinating to see how easy it is to discover what each individual really thinks of himself. Each time someone does this exercise, a single figure immediately exposes his true self-image. He is confronted by his mental limitations, which will match to a tee the limits he will encounter in life. Life will bow before the limits he sets for himself – whether he is aware of this or not. The tragic part is that people who generally fail are the least conscious of these key principles of success and wealth. Conversely, successful individuals have become aware of this phenomenon and done their utmost to work on their self-image.

'The easiest way to do this in the beginning,' he went on, 'is to take a blank sheet of paper and write down steadily larger amounts. One thing is sure in any case. You can't become rich if you aren't convinced that you can. The image you create for yourself must conform to that of a person who can become rich. So let's start our little exercise over again. Write down a much bolder figure this time.'

The young man thought for a few seconds and, squirming uncomfortably, wrote down £60,000, immediately confessing that this was the maximum he could ever hope to earn.

'Maybe it's the maximum you could ever *hope* to earn, but it's definitely not the maximum you could *actually* earn. That's a pretty modest figure. Some people earn it in a month, others in a week, even a day – every day of the year. Let me congratulate you, anyway. You've made astounding progress: you've doubled your self-image and considerably extended your mental boundaries. Not as much as I would have liked, but I don't want to rush you. You have to start by setting yourself an objective that you consider bold but at the same time reasonable. Otherwise it would be too hard for you to believe in it. The secret of a goal is that it must be both ambitious *and* within reach. Never forget this when you finally settle on a goal. On the other hand, don't forget also that most people are over-conservative. They're afraid to make their mental limitations burst wide open. They've turned them into a kind of habit. They're used to living a humdrum existence and going without. They're convinced that that's what life is all about. They're too scared to dream. You musn't be afraid of expanding your mental boundaries. Merely by writing down a series of larger and larger amounts, what you can accomplish in one hour is amazing. Take yourself, for example. You've managed to double your goal within a matter of a few minutes.

'Later on,' he continued, 'when you're alone, do the next exercise. Sit down in the privacy of your bedroom and write out the course of your financial destiny. This is how to do it. Write: in six years to the day I will be a millionaire. This is the practical application of my secret to becoming an instant millionaire. You'll probably object to the fact that it'll take you six long years to become a millionaire. I agree, but it'll take you only a second to activate the secret key that will ensure your financial destiny and fortune.

'As for me, even though I started out with £10,000 that an old millionaire lent me, it took me precisely five years and nine months to make my first million. Ever since then, I've made it prosper by using the same formula each time. This formula has always made many people snigger, and that's not going to change. However, the ones who laugh aren't rich!'

The young man was shaking his head pensively. He didn't really know what to say. He was halfway convinced. But it all seemed a mite too easy.

'Obviously,' continued the Instant Millionaire, 'this formula is valid not only for those who want to become millionaires. After all, not everyone cherishes that ambition. And that's precisely the beauty of this secret. It works equally well for any dreams – from the most modest to the most extravagant. It can make you an extra £5,000 a year or double your income in a year – something that's totally feasible, by the way.

'So, if you don't mind, go and spend some time in your room while I go back to my precious roses, and write the sentence I told you about: in six years to the day, I will be a millionaire. I will therefore be a millionaire on – and then you write the day, the month and the year. Make sure you take note of every single impression that comes into your mind, no matter what it may be. You'll find some paper in the desk. Remember one thing: for as long as you aren't used to the idea of becoming a millionaire, for as long as it isn't an integral part of your life and thus of your innermost thoughts, nothing can help you become a millionaire. Go now and reflect on my formula, which will become your guiding principle during the next six years.'

CHAPTER 8

In which the young man discovers the power of words

A N hour later the butler came to fetch the young man, who hadn't noticed the time pass, so engrossed had he been in the exercise that the eccentric millionaire had given him to do.

The butler explained that the millionaire was expecting him in the garden, and accompanied the young man there in silence. His host was sitting on the bench where he had met him the first day, and was contemplating a freshly cut rose. He raised his head upon hearing the young man approach. He seemed to be in ecstasy, and a gentle smile lit up his face.

'So, how did it go?' he enquired. 'Did the exercise work out all right?'

'Yes, it did. But I've got a lot of questions to ask you.'

'That's what I'm here for.' He invited the young man to sit next to him.

'What bothers me in particular,' he told the old man, 'is that I can't for the life of me see how I can become a millionaire in six years from now even if I do write down this crazy sentence and meditate on it. My question is this: How can I convince myself that I can become a millionaire? I don't even know which field I want to work in. And I still feel I'm pretty young to become a millionaire.'

'That's no obstacle. Countless people became rich at a much younger age than yours. Age isn't a barrier. The major obstacle is not knowing the secret and, when you do know it, not applying it.'

'I'm ready to apply it. The only trouble is that I can't see how I'm ever going to convince myself that I can become a millionaire.'

'There's basically only one way to do it. And it's the same way you used to persuade yourself that you couldn't become a millionaire even if you wanted to. During the next few days, or few weeks at the most, you are going to develop the personality of an instant millionaire. Naturally it's going to take some time to undo everything built up over the years. The secret resides in words, combined with images, which are the special way thoughts express themselves. Each thought you have tends to manifest itself in your life in one way or another. The stronger a person's character is, the more powerful his thoughts will be and the more quickly they will tend to come true, thus shaping the circumstances of his life. This undoubtedly inspired Heraclitus to utter the wise maxim: "Character equals destiny". Desire is what best sustains your thoughts. The more passionate your desire is, the more quickly the thing you want will spring up in your life. The way to become rich is to desire it fervently. In every area of life, sincerity and fervour are the necessary ingredients of success.'

'And yet I sincerely wish to be rich,' said the young man. 'I've been doing everything possible for years now. But nothing's worked out.'

'Ardent desire is necessary, but not enough. What you lack is faith. You must *believe* that you will become a millionaire.'

'How can I get this faith?'

'I've read a great many books on this subject. And what my own master taught me corresponds to the conclusions reached in them. The only way to obtain faith is through the repetition of words. Words have an extraordinary impact on our inner and outer lives. Most people are totally unaware of this principle or fail to use it.... No, I take that back, they do use the power of words, but generally to their detriment. Words are omnipotent.'

'I don't want to contradict you,' said the young man, 'but I think you're exaggerating. I can't really see how words can help me become a millionaire. They might have some importance, but you must agree that it's relative.'

The Instant Millionaire didn't respond to the young man's objection. He was absorbed in his own thoughts. Then he declared: 'In the desk up in your room I left an old booklet that explains this theory in a very enlightening way. Go and find it, please. It's very short. Read it and come down again. We'll continue our discussion later. If you feel the need for more privacy, close your bedroom door.'

The young man agreed. He went back to his room, closed the door and started searching for the booklet in the desk. There was no booklet. However, the young man found a letter that was apparently addressed to him even though it didn't have his name written on it. It was none the less clearly inscribed: LETTER TO A YOUNG MILLIONAIRE.

He opened it. It contained a single word written in red ink: FAREWELL. It was signed: The Instant Millionaire.

The young man's heart began to flutter in his chest like a butterfly gone mad.

At that moment he heard a sound. He turned round and saw a computer that he had never noticed before. Someone must have put it there while he was out. The printer was working. The young man approached it and began to read the printout. It contained one sentence repeated over and over again:

YOU HAVE AN HOUR LEFT TO LIVE.
YOU HAVE AN HOUR LEFT TO LIVE.
YOU HAVE AN HOUR LEFT TO LIVE.
YOU HAVE AN HOUR LEFT TO LIVE.

If this was a joke, it was in bad taste. It had to be a joke, though. Why would the Instant Millionaire want him dead? The young man hadn't done anything to him. But everything was so strange in this place.

Maybe the millionaire was a madman hiding his murderous tendencies behind a veneer of kind-heartedness.

The young man was incredibly confused. He was sure of only one thing: whether or not this was a joke, he certainly wasn't going to take any risks. He was going to make his escape – to forget about his cheque, the secret and the magical theories the millionaire had used to fire up his naïve brain.

He dropped the letter on the floor and made for the door – but it was firmly locked. Panic overtook him. He shook the handle, trying to force the door open, but to no avail. This time the millionaire had gone too far.

The young man went completely berserk. He ran to the window and saw the millionaire working in the garden. Without waiting to wonder if what he was doing made sense, he started yelling at the top of his lungs. No answer. He screamed more loudly. Again no answer. Was the millionaire deaf? He seemed to hear all right up close. The butler then stepped into the garden. The young man called out to him in a loud, hysterical voice, but it was as if he were talking to thin air.

What kind of horrible nightmare was he going through? Both of them couldn't possibly be deaf.

He called again. Another servant appeared a few paces behind the butler. He, too, was completely oblivious to the prisoner's screams for help. The young man was getting more and more desperate by the minute. This surely had to be a devious, well-hatched plot and he had fallen straight into the enemy's hands.

He reconsidered escaping through the window, as he had done the first time he was locked in, but this still looked pretty risky. He'd break his neck. Suddenly, he spotted the telephone. What an idiot he was! Why hadn't he thought of that before? Who could he call? The police? But should he dial the emergency number? What if everything was really all right and they accused him of being a hoaxer?

So he dialled the operator's number. She had a most unusual voice, but when he asked for the nearest police station she gave him a number. Quickly he redialled but he got an engaged signal. What an exasperating sound! He dialled again. Still engaged. It certainly wasn't his day. He tried once more. Suddenly he noticed that the number he was dialling was right before his eyes - not because he had written it down but because it was the one on the telephone he was using. He was calling his own room. He'd been duped!

He tried to force open the door again, but his efforts were to no avail. So he went back to the window. Then he noticed a man approaching the house. He was wearing a vast black cloak and a large, wide-brimmed hat. The young man was almost suffocating with terror. Who could it be but a hired assassin coming to get him? He was trapped like a rat. He was going to die. There was no way out.

Soon footsteps could be heard slowly making their way towards the door. He was right. His time had finally come. He retreated from the door, searching left and right for something to defend himself with. He heard the key turning in the lock. The handle moved, the door opened. There standing in the doorway was a murky black shadow, which swiftly turned into the more substantial figure of a man. Not a word did he say at first. He just stood there, motionless as a statue. Suddenly, he plunged his hand into his pocket. The young man thought he was going to pull out a weapon. Instead, the mysterious, disquieting stranger drew out a letter. At the same time he lifted the brim of his hat and the young man, completely mesmerised, breathlessly expecting the worst, saw under it the millionaire's face filled with malice.

'You forgot your letter in the garden,' said the Instant Millionaire whose disguise now appeared quite amusing to the relieved young man. 'Did you find the booklet I told you about?'

'No, I didn't. I found this instead,' the young man replied, by this time fully reassured by the old man's amiable tone of voice.

He bent down and picked up the letter from the floor.

'What's the meaning of the grotesque scenario you just played out?' demanded the young man. 'I could sue you, you know....'

'But...they're only words, a few words scribbled on a piece of paper. Would you really take me to court for a trifling piece of paper? Didn't you tell me that you didn't believe in the power of words? Look at the state you're in....'

The young man suddenly realised what the millionaire was talking about.

'I just wanted to give you a quick lesson. Experience is a much better teacher than mere theory. Simply put, experience is life. Wasn't that Goethe's philosophy? Grey is the colour of theory; green, the colour of the tree of life.'

'Now do you understand the power that words have?' he went on. 'And another thing: their power is so great that they don't even need to be true to have an effect on people. I assure you that I did not at any time have criminal intentions towards you.'

'How was I to know that?' said the young man, gradually calming down.

'You could have used your head and reasoned things out. Why on earth would I have wanted to kill you? You've never done me any harm. And even if you had, I would never have wished to get even with you. All I want is to be free to tend my rose garden, which is only a pale reflection of the beautiful garden waiting for me. You should have relied on your sense of logic. Yet, did you notice how powerless logic is in a situation such as this? When you were calling to us from the bedroom window and we were pretending not to hear, you were truly in despair. The mistake you made wasn't reading a threat that was sheer fabrication, but believing in it. By doing so you instinctively obeyed one of the greatest laws governing the human mind. When imagination and logic are in conflict with each other, the imagination almost invariably takes over. Your worst mistake was losing your head over a threat that wasn't even aimed at you.'

The millionaire then went up to the printer, stopped it and tore out the sheet. He showed it to the young man, who was aghast that he hadn't even noticed that the threat had nothing to do with him. At the top of the page was written a stranger's name. The young man felt rather ashamed. He had got all worked up over a mere figment of his imagination.

CHAPTER 9

*In which the young man is first shown
the heart of the rose*

'YOU'VE learned many important things today,'
the millionaire told the young man. 'And you've
understood them not only with your head but with
your heart as well. Now you know that words can
deeply affect our lives whether we wish it or not. You
weren't even the target of the threat that was printed
out by the computer, and yet you were needlessly
scared out of your wits.... But not really needlessly, in
fact, since you learned a valuable lesson. A thought,
even when false, can affect us if we believe it to be
true. But when we learn to distinguish the value of a
thought, that is to say, the value we give it, our mind
regains or maintains its calm. It was your mind, in
fact, that gave meaning to the threat, for if it had been
written in a foreign language that you didn't understand you wouldn't have paid the slightest attention to
it.'

To give the young man time to grasp what he was
getting at, the millionaire fell silent. A moment later
he continued, 'In the future, each time you come face

to face with a problem – and the road to fortune is strewn with obstacles – remember this threat. Tell yourself that the problem facing you has as little to do with you as that threat did. This might seem excessive to you, since you're the one who has to deal with the problem. Just make sure that someone else shoulders the anxiety it breeds. Aim it in another direction. I don't know if I'm making myself clear. Never let a problem acquire so much importance in your eyes that it traumatises you. By the time you have reached this point – and it's not easy, I assure you – you will have mastered an invaluable skill and will be able to fulfil all your dreams. Let me warn you, however. The journey will be long and arduous before you do manage to master it. But never give up. I promise you, it'll be worth your while. Hopefully, one day, you might even learn that that is the ultimate purpose of life. The rest is unimportant.'

After delivering his message, the millionaire remained silent. He seemed absorbed in his thoughts. Sadness filled his eyes. Nevertheless he added a few more words, as if they were the conclusion to everything he had said up to that point: 'Life can be a rose garden or hell on earth, depending on your frame of mind. Think of the rose. Lose yourself in the heart of a rose each time a problem crops up. And remember the threat that was aimed at someone else. If you want them to, problems will always be directed towards someone else.'

He placed particular emphasis on the following words: 'Most people cannot understand what I've just said. They believe it to be pure, unadulterated optimism. But it's much more profound than that. It's one of the major principles of the mind. For those unable to see evil, evil does not exist. The world is but a reflection of your inner self. The conditions in your life are but a mirror image of your inner life. If you have no weakness, nothing that attracts problems or evil, then evil cannot touch you nor can danger threaten you. Constantly reaffirm the principle that evil doesn't exist, and concentrate on the heart of the rose. Here you will find truth and the intuition that you will need to guide you through life. You will also find that thing so rare on earth: love for whatever you do, and love for others. That is the dual secret of true wealth.'

CHAPTER 10

In which the young man learns to master his unconscious mind

AFTER this long and heartfelt statement the elderly millionaire seemed to be exhausted, and fell silent for several minutes. Then he continued, carefully stressing each word, 'That's why the formula I gave you is so powerful. Even if at the beginning you believe it highly unlikely that you will ever become a millionaire, you *will* be able to become one. Just do the same thing with the formula that you did with the letter. Accept what it is saying as the truth, for the greatest secret of all successful achievements is believing. If you have faith that you will be able to accomplish something, you will.'

'My only problem is believing that I can become a millionaire in five years from now. In the case of the letter I let myself be tricked - I lost my head. But this formula is a different matter altogether.'

'Even if you don't believe in the formula, it'll begin acting on you. The more you internalise it, the more powerful it will become. The advantage is that it's not your reasoning or conscious mind that you must convince. Remember the threat. It seemed absurd to you, and with reason. But it was stronger than you, so to speak. Part of you - your imagination - accepted it as real. And the imagination is what some people call the unconscious mind. It is the hidden part of your mind, and much more powerful than the visible part. It guides your entire life. I could spend hours talking to you about the theory of the unconscious. But it's enough for you to know that the unconscious is extremely susceptible to the power of words. Now do you know why you are having so much difficulty believing the highly plausible and realisable fact that you can become a millionaire in less than six years?'

'Sorry. I don't.'

'Well, the fact remains that for years and years sentences and thoughts - thus words - have been engraving themselves in your unconscious. Deeply. In fact every experience, every thought you've ever had, every word you've ever heard has become indelibly etched in your unconscious. In the long run this prodigious memory becomes a person's self-image. Without your realising it, your past experiences and the inner monologue you hold with yourself have convinced you that you aren't the type of person who can become a millionaire, even if, objectively speaking, you have all the qualities to do so and more easily than you can imagine. Like everyone else, your self-image is so powerful that it unwittingly becomes your destiny. Outer circumstances end up matching the image you have of yourself with amazing precision. To become rich, you have to create a new self-image for yourself.'

'I'm sure I can, but that still doesn't solve my problem. I'm quite willing to accept all these theories. The only snag is that I can't see how I'm going to convince myself that I can become a millionaire.'

'It's easy, don't you see? Think about the threat a little while ago. It wasn't true, yet it affected you as if it were. All you have to do is play the same trick on yourself. Your unconscious won't be any the wiser for it. When you were a child - and even later than that - each time you accepted a suggestion, even though it was false, you basically tricked your unconscious. In any case, you forced it to accept something that was patently untrue. So now you're going to do the same thing. Your unconscious can be influenced at will. And once it has been influenced in the sense you meant it to be, which is basically child's play, you will be able to obtain exactly what you want out of life. Why? Because your unconscious will be convinced that you *can* obtain all these things. It will accept them as true in the same way that it's now accepting the fact that you can't get more. This ties in with what I said earlier on. Man is the reflection of the thoughts stored in his unconscious.'

Sensing that the young man was getting more and more interested in what he was saying, the millionaire decided to go on. 'The most important thing is to pretend that something is true. Why does this work with the unconscious? Simply because, though the unconscious may be powerful, it cannot discriminate between truth and falsehood. Think back to the threat you received this morning. Your unconscious wasn't able to differentiate between what was and wasn't objectively true. And it reacted in a very specific way. If your mind hadn't accepted the suggestion contained in this letter - if it had, in a manner of speaking, closed the door to the unconscious - you would not have had the violent reaction that you did. You'd have stayed perfectly calm and waited until the situation cleared itself up.'

'Yes, but what happens if there's a conflict between my conscious and my unconscious? What happens if my conscious mind refuses to accept the idea of wealth?'

'The only solution, besides being the best and undoubtedly the quickest, is repetition.'

'Repetition?'

'That's right. This technique is commonly called self-suggestion. Each one of us is subject to it throughout our lives. Every day we are influenced by inner and outer suggestions. The inner monologue that all of us continually hold with ourselves shapes our lives. Some of us repeat to ourselves that we will never be successful because we come from a family of losers, or because we have had failures that appear definitive in our eyes. So we drift from failure to failure, not because we don't have the necessary qualities to succeed, but because that's how we unconsciously picture ourselves.

'Some men believe they can never attract women,' the millionaire continued, 'and yet they simply ooze charm. For some reason or other, women flee them like the plague. The power of their self-image, which is the reflection of the unconscious, is again responsible for this. It brings about the kind of circumstances that make women run away from such people.

'But the repetition of negative formulas,' he ended up, 'which have such a tremendous impact on our lives, can be used in a different way. And that's what we're going to do. The unconscious is a slave that can dominate us because it is immensely powerful. But it is also blind, and you have to learn how to play tricks on it.'

It would be too much to say that the young man understood everything the millionaire was saying, and yet the overall impression he was getting seemed positive to him. He felt that the old man was putting a finger on his problem, and he was eager to find out more.

'The beauty of this theory is that you don't really have to believe in it to use it,' the millionaire said. 'But to get results you have to put it to use - they won't come magically on their own. Yet the secret is simple: everything, as I've said, depends on repetition. Even if you don't believe it at first, try it - at least for a couple of days. That's long enough for you to start feeling its effects.

'This formula might appear simple,' he went on, 'not to mention simplistic, to you, but let me tell you that it is the most potent secret on the face of the earth. Remember the first words of the Bible: "In the beginning was the Word." The Word, meaning speech. Self-suggestion plays a major role in our lives. If you remain unaware of it, it will work against you more often than not. Conversely, if you decide to use it, all its tremendous power will be put at your disposal.'

'Well, I think you've convinced me - although, to tell you the truth, I still don't understand a lot of things about this theory,' said the young man.

'All right. Now, here's what you have to do. Once again it might appear too easy to you at first, but you must base your judgement on the results you get rather than on intellectual criteria....'

CHAPTER 11

In which the young man and his mentor discuss figures and formulas

THE millionaire now sat down at the desk and invited the young man to join him. He took out some paper and a pen and lined up some figures. 'Your formula could look like this,' he explained. What he had written was: By the end of this year I will possess assets worth £31,250. I will double those assets every year for five years, then (and here he left a space) I will be a millionaire.

'You mustn't confuse assets and income,' he told the young man. 'Your assets are whatever you have left over after your taxes and current bills are paid up. They could comprise property investments, company shares or savings in a bank or building society. Now if you want to be a millionaire in six years - which is the realistic objective I'm proposing - your formula will have to be set up on this model. If you have assets worth £31,250 by the end of the first year, you will have to double them each year. And in six years you will be a millionaire!

'Why double your assets each year? Because it's a simple operation that your subconscious can easily handle. And it's easier for you to remember. It also guarantees you constant growth. As such, you won't be taking the risk of waiting for the seventh year to become a millionaire.

'Moreover,' he went on, 'this formula is virtually obligatory if you want to be a millionaire within a period as short as six years. But you might not be able to achieve assets totalling £31,250 by the end of the first year that you can double the second year.

'If this starting point appears too ambitious to you, then give yourself another year. Becoming a million-aire in seven years is still pretty good! Your goal for the first year will then be £15,625. Believe me when I tell you it's far from being beyond reach. And if you're convinced that you can have a cosy nest egg worth £15,625 by the end of the first year, you will have it.

'Now if that still seems over-ambitious, give your-self yet another year, making eight. Then the goal for your first year will be £7,812.50.

'With your formula: I WILL BE A MILLION-AIRE ON (then you put the month and year, in five, seven or ten years' time), you will also have to set yourself short-term objectives, landmarks to help motivate you during your journey on the road to rich-es. And, of course, an annual goal is fundamental.

'The most important thing, however,' he told his pupil, 'is to write your goals down on paper. Take a pencil and fool around with figures and years. Don't be afraid. It can't do you any harm. The amounts will become more and more familiar to you as you play around with them. Thousands of people want to get rich, and yet not one out of a hundred takes the initiative to outline the route he intends to take to reach his goal. Be different! Set up your plans and charts. Work out projections until you've found the plan that suits you. It'll be your plan. For inspiration use the examples I've provided, but then let your imagination run wild. You have to start by dreaming to get rich. You have to know how to quantify your dream, translating it into sums of money and dates. This, in fact, should be the first exercise you do. Juggle numbers. You will soon see that this little game reveals who you really are.

'The simple fact of putting your goals, deadlines and sums on paper is the first step towards transforming your ideal into its material equivalent.

'Anyone who wants to stick to an ambition to become a millionaire in five or ten years must take note of this fact: if he is currently earning £20,000 a year and can expect nothing more than, say, an annual 10 per cent rise, then he'll never become a millionaire if he remains in his job unless he also has sideline activities.

'There's nothing dramatic or reprehensible in this as far as it goes. It's purely an objective observation. The formula of doubling your fortune each year or increasing your assets with respect to the previous year's is clearly not the only way to become a million-aire. However, the secret it contains - that is, a quanti-fied goal (an amount and a deadline by which to reach it) - is valid for anyone wishing to succeed.

'For example, you might simply want to increase your income by £5,000 a year. If you now earn £25,000, you would probably like to earn £30,000 - a matter of affording a few more luxuries. Or perhaps you are earning £30,000 and would like £40,000 to enable you to trade up from your present house with-out worrying about the extra mortgage payments. And you might also be able to afford a new car, one that is a little more luxurious.

'To do this, the formula is just as easy. Simply repeat to yourself: THIS YEAR I WILL INCREASE MY INCOME BY £5,000 or £10,000 AND I WILL EARN £30,000 or £40,000 (as the case may be).

'You don't need to know how you'll manage it. You simply have to realise that if all you can hope for is a 10 per cent annual pay rise in your present job, and you don't want to moonlight, you will have to land a promotion or switch jobs to reach your goal. This may appear self-evident, but thousands of people hope to improve their material situation and do absolutely nothing about it. Is this ignorance? Is it because they are basically satisfied with their situa-tions even though they complain day in and day out?

'Once you've observed that you need a change in your life to reach your aim, you might tell yourself that you have nothing in sight. And you might wonder how the devil you're going to earn that extra £5,000 or £10,000 that you need. Not to worry. This isn't a serious dilemma. What counts is fully to permeate your unconscious with your goal, duly written down, stating such and such an amount and deadline. Your unconscious will do the rest. Stay on your toes. And since you've become aware that things won't get better on their own, when an opportunity or lucky break crops up grab it without the slightest hesitation. Don't let yourself be paralysed by fear, which prevents so many people from living out their dreams. You know that by doing nothing you won't get your rise. So you mustn't hesitate to take the steps necessary to achieve your goal.

'Correctly programmed, your unconscious will work wonders for you. If you've issued it the order to increase your income by £10,000, it will definitely execute it. Remind it daily, so that this mission becomes its magnificent obsession. Like a remote-control missile, it will overcome all the obstacles standing in its way to hit its target. Your job is to arrange all the details correctly.

'What is the target?' he continued. 'When must the explosion take place? The target is £10,000 and the explosion date the end of the year. Such are the magical powers of the unconscious and a quantified objective.

'When creating your objectives, keep in mind that most people are over-cautious. Why? Because they don't believe they're worth anything. Their self-image is rock-bottom.' At this point in his lecture, the millionaire saw fit to illustrate his theory with a short personal anecdote.

'A few years ago,' he whispered confidentially to the young man, 'I was thinking of hiring a managing director for one of my companies. I worked out that I'd be ready to offer him £45,000. When the time came to talk salary, he told me in a rather dry, nervous, almost imperious voice: "I won't accept anything below £30,000."

'After a lengthy pause I said, as if I were making a major concession: "Given your background, £30,000 is fine by me."

'If he had asked for £35,000, I'd have given it to him. The same goes for £40,000 and even £45,000, since that was what I was willing to give him even before the interview. Besides, the way the interview went had pleased me so much that I might even have bumped that amount up to £50,000.

'So the person I took on had himself lost £20,000 in a matter of minutes. That's a lot of money. Just think - it totals £200,000 in the first ten years alone!

'Why did he forfeit this money? Simply because he didn't believe he was worth £50,000 a year. I must admit that, after hearing him state his salary expectations, I hesitated for a fraction of a second and was about to send him away without the job. He himself was in the best position to assess his own worth, and he was telling me that his managerial skills were worth only £30,000 while I was looking for someone worth £45,000. Was I making the wrong choice? The future proved that I'd made the right choice by taking him, and I saved a lot of money. His problem was that he lacked self-confidence and under-rated what he was really worth. He gradually dealt with this problem over the years - which cost me a bundle in salary increases. But they were worth it....

'What you should remember from this simple example is that I dealt with this manager just as life deals with each one of us. Life gives us exactly what we expect from it. No more, no less. We tend to forget, however, that it is generally ready to give us much more than we realise or are used to asking for.

'I've talked a lot,' concluded the millionaire. 'What do you make of all this, young man?'

'It seems too good to be true,' he objected, even though he had hung on to every word the millionaire had uttered.

'Yet this simple little method, and none other,' he responded, 'is exactly what helped turn me into a millionaire and has done the same for all those I've shared it with. Words are extremely powerful agents. The stronger your character becomes, the more the words you utter will become genuine decrees. Everything you affirm, fuelled by deep inner conviction and strengthened by the fires of repetition, will take shape more and more quickly.'

'Hearing you outline your theory makes me wonder whether this is nothing but a game,' the young man interrupted him.

'Perhaps. Only you have to do the exercise. Nobody can do it for you. You must repeat your formula aloud day and night at least fifty times. And more if you can. Even a hundred times a day. This is an exercise in itself. The first few times I laid down and counted by tapping my fingers on the floor, five times with both hands.'

'You have to admit that it takes practice.'

'At first you'll find that it won't necessarily be easy. The mind is prone to wander. After repeating it ten times, you'll start thinking of something else. Bring your mind back to business and start at zero again until you manage to reach fifty. If you can't stick to such an elementary form of discipline, you'd better give up your dream of becoming rich.... That's the challenge I'm offering you, my friend. And I know you can do it. All you need to do is to persist.'

'Why repeat the formula aloud?'

'This will affect your mind even more strongly. The order you are issuing to your unconscious will seem as though it is coming from the outside, and will thus sound more imperious. Say it in a monotone, well modulated and articulated. Pronounce the formula like an incantation or a mantra, as the Buddhists call it. In time the formula will acquire its own life.'

The young man was impressed with what the millionaire was telling him. The old man was no longer smiling. He was speaking seriously, somewhat like an oracle.

'At first, you might feel a little embarrassed by the sound of your voice and by the formula you'll be repeating. But gradually you'll get used to it. The goal you laid out for yourself, which seemed audacious at first, will appear attainable and even ridiculously easy.'

'Don't you think that at certain moments I might be tempted to start giggling at the absurdity of it all?'

'It's during those moments more than at any other time that you must persist. You must conquer your doubt. Think of me. I'll be with you every instant, even if I'm in my other garden far away from here. And my forces will be with you. In your moments of doubt, remember that I've given you my word. You will succeed.'

'You're sure about that?' asked the young man, still not totally convinced.

'Why would I have any doubts about it? You'll become an instant millionaire like I did. Besides, you've already become one now that you understand and accept the principle. The secret law of life is that anyone who understands the true principle obtains power. Knowing it will bring you freedom. It's only a matter of time before you become a millionaire in reality. You are already one in your mind, and that's what is most important of all.'

'But I have scarcely a penny to my name....'

'So keep repeating the secret formula. Little by little you will see a change occurring within you. Your goal will seem more and more natural. It'll become part of your life in just the same way that the narrow image you have had of yourself until now has seemed to be an integral part of your being, even though it was only a well-worn figment of your imagination. What your mind conjured up in the past can be reformulated in a new way. As such, you will be able to mould your future the way you want it - you will at last become master of your own destiny. Isn't that everyone's secret dream, even if they don't admit it?'

The young man agreed. He was overwhelmed with emotion. It seemed to him that the old man's words had much greater significance than he had believed at first. Of course his methods were a bit strange. But who cared so long as they worked?

CHAPTER 12

In which the young man learns about happiness and life

'TO help and support you,' the Instant Millionaire told his young disciple, 'I'm now going to give you another, more general formula. You will derive enormous benefits from it throughout your life. It will transform you inside and out. In fact, it will enable you to acquire true wealth - which isn't only the acquisition of material possessions. It's much less specific than that. It's a mental attitude towards life.

'Let me give you some advice,' he continued. 'Of course your money formula will allow you to achieve and probably even top your financial objectives. However, during your search for wealth never lose sight of the fact that, if you lose happiness, you lose everything. The pursuit of money can easily turn into an obsession preventing you from enjoying life. As the famous saying goes: "What shall it profit a man, if he shall gain the whole world, and lose his own soul?" This question might bring a smile to the lips of those who find it too metaphysical or religious. But it's my belief that money is an excellent servant but a tyranni-cal master.'

'Do you mean that happiness and money can't co-exist?'

'Far from it, but you must stay very alert not to let it take over your mind. John D. Rockefeller, who was the richest man in the world, was so preoccupied, so crushed by the weight of his worries, that at the age of fifty he was a little old man and, in a manner of speak-ing, condemned to die. His stomach was so out of order that all it could stand was bread and milk. He lived in constant fear of losing his money and being betrayed by his associates. Money had become his master and he couldn't even enjoy it any more. In a way he was poorer than a simple office clerk who could enjoy a good meal.'

'At the same time that you're dangling wealth in front of my eyes,' said the young man, 'you have the gift of frightening me.'

'That's not my intention, though,' replied the mil-lionaire, 'and the formula I'm about to give you will help you avoid walking into the trap into which most fortune-seekers have fallen. People who are still basi-cally poor work relentlessly to achieve their ends. The first money they earn triggers their deep-seated ambi-tion, causing them to crave more and more. And when they start earning big money they suddenly become afraid of losing it.

'My formula is simple. It is a variation of the famous formula devised by the physician Émile Coué, for patients in his clinic: EVERY DAY, IN EVERY WAY, I AM GETTING BETTER AND BETTER. Repeat this formula aloud fifty times, morning and evening, and as many times as you can during the day. The more often you repeat it, the greater the impact it will have on you.'

The inexperienced young man was all ears listening to the wise old man, who was seeing his life pass before his eyes, a life that had been full and for the most part happy. The young man felt that standing before him was the first happy man he had ever met in his life.

'Most people want to be happy,' continued the millionaire, 'but they don't know what they're looking for. So inevitably they die without ever having found it. And even if they did find it, since they don't know what they're looking for, how would they ever recognise it? They're exactly like the people hunting for wealth whom we talked about yesterday. They truly wanted to be rich. But when you ask them abruptly how much they'd like to earn in a year, most of them are incapable of answering. When you don't know where you're going, you generally get nowhere.'

This made perfect sense to the young man. It was so disarmingly simple. Why on earth hadn't he ever thought of that before? Probably because he'd never taken the time to stop and think about it. That was his mistake. A lack of thinking. He vowed then and there that in the future he would do a lot more thinking about things. That would prevent a lot of mistakes.

'Happiness, of course, has been defined in a million different ways,' the millionaire proceeded to say. 'For each one of us, even for those of us who have thought about it, it translates into a wide variety of things. But I'll give you the key to happiness. It isn't a definition, so it applies to everybody. With this key you will be able to know beyond a shadow of a doubt at any time of your life if you are happy. And especially if you are doing what it takes to make you happy. I must warn you that what I'm going to say might surprise you at first, and might even seem a little sad and morbid to you. Ask yourself: If I were to die tonight, could I tell myself at the instant of my death that I had accomplished everything I had set out to do that day?'

The young man raised his eyebrows. 'I don't understand,' he confessed.

'When you have done exactly what your inner self feels you should do each day, you will feel free to leave the world each day. However, to be perfectly sure that you are doing what you should be doing, you will have to do what you love doing. People who don't do what they enjoy are not happy. They spend their time daydreaming about what they would like to be doing. And since they never actually do what they dream about, they are inevitably unhappy. And when people aren't happy, they aren't ready to die at a moment's notice.'

'I've barely started living, and here you go talking to me about death as if it were just a stone's throw away,' anxiously replied the young man.

'I must honestly admit that this philosophy may at first glance seem like a philosophy of death. And yet it's a philosophy of life, one hundred per cent. Those who never do what they really enjoy doing, who have given up their dreams, so to speak, belong to the living dead. To understand this philosophy, ask yourself that question again and answer it with total sincerity. If you lie, you'll only be lying to yourself, and you become the loser in this game. If you knew you were going to die tomorrow, wouldn't you change your plans for today? Wouldn't you do something else with your life rather than what you've been doing up to now?'

'I'm not quite sure, sir.'

'You'd probably start by making the necessary arrangements: you'd make a will, if you hadn't already, and say goodbye to your family and friends. But let's suppose that all of these earthly tasks took only one hour, what would you do with the remaining twenty-three? Ask that question of everybody you know. Their responses will invariably fall into two categories. Unhappy people who don't enjoy their lives will tell you that they'd do something totally different. And you wouldn't need to wonder whether they were telling the truth. Why on earth would they continue doing something they hated if they had only twenty-four hours left to live?

'The second category,' the millionaire continued, 'and unfortunately it's the minority, would do exactly what they normally do every day of their lives. Why would they change that? Their work is their passion. Isn't it quite understandable that they would do it till their time was up? Why would they start doing something they didn't like? Bach belonged to this category. On his deathbed he was correcting the last piece of music he'd written. But you don't have to be a genius to want to work until the end. Each one of us in our own way and in our own occupation can become a genius, even if unrecognised by society. To be a genius simply means to do what you enjoy doing. That is the true genius of life. Mediocrity is never daring to do what you love - for fear of what others will say, for fear of losing your security.'

'A security which is an illusion more often than not, isn't it?' timidly ventured the young man.

'That's right. So ask yourself the question: If I were to die tomorrow, what would I do with the last hours of my life? Would I continue doing a job that is killing me deep down since it has nothing to do with my real aspirations? Would I agree to go on being a shadow of my true self, totally lacking in self-respect, since I'm forcing myself to do something I hate? Imagine that you invite a friend over to your house to help you do some chores. Would you give the dirtiest ones to your friend? Of course not. So why force on yourself tasks that you find so degrading? Why are you your own worst enemy? Why not become your own best friend?'

Silence followed these words.

The old millionaire then went on: 'And what would *you* do if you were to die tomorrow? Would you do exactly what you've been doing?'

'No, I wouldn't,' the young man was forced to admit.

'That means that you're probably not happy. Now, consider the following observation. Don't you find it highly presumptuous to believe that you *won't* die tomorrow?'

Upon hearing these words, the young man felt troubled. Over the past few days the old man had often displayed an uncanny ability to see into the future. Was he now announcing his imminent death? In a roundabout way, perhaps, but clearly enough.

The millionaire seemed to read his thoughts. After all, the young man's uneasiness was rather visible.

'Don't worry,' he said, amused, 'you're not going to die tomorrow. You'll live to a ripe old age.... But allow me to pursue my line of reasoning. Let's take a more general case this time. You'll feel less affected than by these morbid arguments. When you look at life through your mind's eye, death will acquire another meaning. But we haven't reached that point yet, have we? Don't you find it presumptuous of people to believe that they always have their entire lives ahead of them? In many cases, death strikes out of the blue. People, however, rely on the certainty - or rather the illusion - that they have lots of time ahead of them, allowing them constantly to put off the decisions they should make. They tell themselves: "I've got time. I'll get down to business later". Old age arrives and they find they haven't done anything yet.'

'That's probably why we say, "If youth only knew, if old age only could",' said the young man.

'That's true, alas! The secret of happiness, therefore, is to live as if each day were your last. And to live each day to the fullest by doing what you feel you should be doing and what you would do if your hours were numbered. Because, basically, they are. But we always seem to realise this when there's very little time left. Then it's too late. So you must be courageous enough to act immediately. Live with this thought in mind: "I refuse to die without having had the courage to do what I wanted to do. I do not want to die with the appalling thought that society tricked me, that it got the better of me and annihilated my dreams". You must not die with the dreadful feeling that your fears were stronger than your dreams and that you never discovered what you really enjoyed. You must know how to dare.'

'I agree with your ideas. What I mean is that I think they make a lot of sense. But what happens if I'm not absolutely sure that I don't really like what I'm doing? I don't know of any occupation that is completely free of hassles. If everything were perfect, we wouldn't be here.'

'You're absolutely right. Even a profession that fires us up has its negative aspects. Another way to find out whether your job really pleases you is to ask yourself this question: "If I had a million pounds in the bank tomorrow, would I continue doing the same job?" Obviously if your answer is no, you don't really like it. Tell me, how many people would keep up the same occupation if they suddenly became millionaires? The truth is that they are few and far between. Besides, those who would answer yes to this question are generally already millionaires. Otherwise they'd retire early or do something else. But most of the millionaires I know refuse to retire, and go on working very late in life. I'd even go so far as to say that all millionaires, excluding those who married into or inherited their fortunes, are that way precisely because they loved their work.

'My reasoning has just come full circle,' he continued. 'To become a millionaire, or at least rich, you must enjoy your occupation. Those who stay in a job they hate are doubly penalised. Not only does their work weigh them down but, worse still, it doesn't even make them wealthy. In fact, most people spend their lives in this strange paradox. Why? Because they are unaware of the genuine laws of success. And because of fear. They waste their lives and their chances of becoming truly rich by clinging to a type of security that is mediocre at best. They believe wealth is reserved to others, or that they are talentless. And why do they let themselves be tricked into believing this illusion? Because their minds are not strong enough to see reality, to glimpse the truth of this illusion. Remember the maxim: "Character equals destiny." Strengthen your mind and circumstances will yield to your desires. You will control your own life.'

'Have you always been happy?' asked the young man.

'Frankly, no. There were times when I was utterly miserable. The thought of committing suicide even crossed my mind. Until the day when I, too, met an eccentric millionaire who taught me almost everything I'm telling you today. At first, however, I was pretty sceptical. I couldn't believe that this theory could apply in my case, even though he was living proof that it worked. In the end, since I had tried all sorts of things and was still unsuccessful, and since I had nothing to lose, I was willing to give it a try. I was thirty and I felt I was wasting my life. It seemed as if things were slipping through my fingers.'

'I'm sure that today you don't regret having applied the advice the eccentric old man gave you.'

'He often repeated that I could become the master of my life and control all the events taking place in it. I never believed him. It seemed like science fiction. Then, one day, by dint of hearing him repeat the same song over and over again, I told myself that maybe he was right, that maybe life was not what I'd always thought it was - a series of more or less unpredictable and uncontrollable events in which luck and fate were king. I felt that we could perhaps control our destinies if we started by mastering the mind. I noticed that I was beginning to think like that - in other words, that a revolution was taking place in my mind - only after I'd spent quite some time repeating the formula he had passed down to me: EVERY DAY, IN EVERY WAY, I AM GETTING BETTER AND BETTER.

'My mentor also taught me another formula, which in my opinion is even more powerful - at least as far as my own experience goes. Naturally I wholeheartedly recommend it to you. True, it's slightly religious in nature, which will probably put some people off. That's a pity, since it has an invaluable effect on the mind. Repeating this formula has calmed me down when I felt anxious or nervous and has brought me answers when I seriously needed them. Tranquillity is the greatest manifestation of power. Look at the mighty and powerful: they are calm. And what is the symbol of supreme power? God, of course. That's one of the reasons why the formula I'm about to give you is so effective: BE STILL THEN, AND KNOW THAT I AM GOD.

'Repeat it every day as often as you can. It will bring you that feeling of serenity, so necessary for getting through life's upheavals. When my mentor decided to reveal it to me he announced it by saying that, of all the secrets in the world, this one was the most precious. That was his spiritual legacy to me, as it is mine to you. That should convince you of the power of this formula.'

'I hope you're not turning into a preacher,' responded the young man, 'but I do understand your message.'

'By repeating this formula,' said the old man, 'which seemed strange to me at first, I developed a new inner power. This power, which never ceased growing over the years, kept reminding me of something the old millionaire had repeated to me over and over again: I COULD DO ANYTHING, nothing would be impossible for me as soon as I became the master of my destiny. So, little by little, I convinced myself that I could steer my life exactly where I wanted it to go. I've continued applying the formula and have done what my mentor asked me to do. I want you to do the same thing, too.'

CHAPTER 13

In which the young man learns to express his desires in life

'YOU have already taken the first step,' explained the millionaire. 'It was getting down the formula and the quantified objective: an amount and a deadline. Now for the second step: take a sheet of paper and write down everything you want out of life. Your dream must be precise if you want it to take shape. This is what I started out asking for.

'The following financial goals within five years:
- ☐ A house worth £300,000.
- ☐ A second home in the country worth £150,000.
- ☐ An old, retuned Mercedes worth £20,000.
- ☐ A new BMW worth £30,000.
- ☐ No more personal debts.
- ☐ £200,000 in cash and other liquid assets.
- ☐ £200,000 invested in the stock market and other investments.
- ☐ £300,000 invested in property worth six times as much as at the time of purchase.

'My non-financial objectives were:

☐ Two-week holidays at least three times a year, when ever I felt like taking them.

☐ To be my own boss and not work more than thirty hours a week.

☐ Intelligent, rich friends involved in business and art.

☐ A loving and charming wife and beautiful children, allowing me to have a fulfilling family life.

☐ A maid and cook to free us of everyday tasks.

The young man was flabbergasted by the picture the Instant Millionaire had just drawn.

'It looks too good to be true, doesn't it?' said the millionaire. 'I too thought that I'd gone a bit overboard by the time I'd finished outlining what I wanted. But my hesitation and fears were due merely to a negative mental attitude and to my ingrained habit of thinking small. I was doing this without even realising it.

'However,' he went on, 'sketching out a list like this is exactly the way to discover your narrow vision of things. Those who consider this kind of life plan unachievable simply think small since, everything being relative under the sun, this ambition is hardly exorbitant. The proof is that the rich would be exceedingly unhappy if they had to make do with the paltry conditions which I have just sketched out. Many of them live in houses worth a million, employ dozens of servants and own a private plane, an island in the South Seas, racehorses and so on and so forth. Do they find that their lifestyles are blown up out of all proportion? Hardly. They don't even think they're rich. In any case not that rich, since they always have friends or business associates with more money than them. Why do they find this kind of lifestyle normal? Well, either they were born rich, or they thought big and managed to raise themselves to this status and achieve their dreams. None of them ever believed that he couldn't do it. If you start out with the idea that you can't, you are blocking yourself straightaway. So do this exercise. Write down what you want out of life in minute detail, without holding anything back.

'It will show you the limits of your ambitions, and your mental limits. What are you really dreaming of? What would you be satisfied with? It's important to fill in as many details as possible. The only thing to avoid is choosing your dream home at a fixed address, because this house may never become available. You'd be running the risk of never seeing your dream come true despite the power of your desire and will, or perhaps because your dream is contrary to the order of things or is harmful to others - something which should always be taken into consideration.

'This portrait will show you who you really are. It will become the concrete shape of your desires. Your thoughts are shapes. They are alive. Each thought which is expressed tends to come true. The more specific it is, the better the chances are for it to materialise.

Hence the importance of details. In mysterious and unexpected ways these thoughts, nourished regularly, will bring about the circumstances allowing them to come true.'

Since the young man was looking sceptical at this point, the millionaire added: 'I know that all this seems Utopian. But as I told you, the stronger your mind becomes, the more you will realise that there's nothing it can't accomplish. Besides, all you have to do is think about the power that enabled Jesus Christ to perform miracles like resurrecting the dead. Don't you find that, comparatively speaking, realising a dream as ordinary as having a £300,000 house is rather a banal achievement? Don't you believe that the mind is much more powerful than ordinary people think and, above all, believe it to be? Remember what Christ said: "Faith moves mountains."'

The young man was stunned into silence.

'To use your mind effectively, you must start believing in its power. In any case, you must be favourably biased towards it. You have to give the runner a chance. So draw up your list. Don't you feel even at this stage that it's rather low-key and attainable by comparison with a resurrection? Don't you understand by now that you can achieve such simple things in your life?'

'I need time to think,' protested the young man.

'Good idea. Think about what I've just told you. Part of you believes in what I'm saying. The other part is blindfolded and gagged because of years of faulty education and unfortunate experiences - but it's still alive. It's only waiting for a sign from you to wake it up. To become the lord and master of your existence instead of a tormented slave helplessly buffeted by events, listen to that tiny inner voice sleeping in the depths of your mind and give it more freedom to express itself. The more often you repeat the formula, the more powerful it will become and the more surely it will guide you. This is your intuition, the voice of your soul. The road to your secret power.'

The young man felt a bit dizzy and was ready to take a break.

'Come,' said the millionaire, 'Let's take a walk in the garden to relax. I'd love to take my last walk here with a friend.'

These sombre words saddened the young man. It wasn't the first time the millionaire had made such an allusion...as if knowing that death was close at hand.

CHAPTER 14

In which the young man discovers the secrets of the rose garden

THE two men walked through the garden in silence. The millionaire stopped in front of a rose bush laden with magnificent flowers, and seemed lost in contemplation. Then, straightening up, he said: 'I must have smelled these roses thousands of times, and yet each time it's a different experience. Do you know why? Because I've learned to live in the here and now. Forgetful of the past, unmindful of the future. The secret is extremely simple. It resides in mental concentration. The harder your mind is concentrating, the more it lives in the present, the more it is absorbed in what it is doing. Concentration is the key to success in all facets of life. The better you are able to concentrate, the more quickly and efficiently you will be able to work. You will spot details that others overlook.'

'Have all rich and successful people learned to pay attention to details?'

'They have indeed. By increasing your own powers of concentration, you will be able to make wise observations on things. You will learn to judge accurately the people you meet. Your powers of concentration will enable you to discover at a glance who they really are. And you will become realistic in the truest sense of the word. Or, at least, in its deepest sense. You will see things as they are. That hazy film of thoughts and daydreams found in the majority of people will no longer block your vision of things. Constantly distracted, most people go through life like sleepwalkers. They see neither the things nor the people they meet. They live as if in a dream. They are never in the present. Therefore, properly speaking, they are never there. Their mistakes and failures haunt them. Their minds are permeated with fears of the future.'

'As far as I can see it, concentration seems to be the easiest link in your theory.'

'Be careful, young man. Not everyone who tries it succeeds. But when your mind reaches a proper level of concentration, your ability to solve problems will become formidable. You won't become negligent, just realistic. Instead of wasting your nervous energy biting your nails over your worries, you'll apply yourself to solving them. Don't forget that being over-anxious and worrying yourself to death about a problem has never solved anything. On the other hand, it has provoked many a stomach ulcer and heart attack. The image you have of yourself will change. Each human being is an enigma. The problem is that we are all enigmas not only to others, but to ourselves as well. This comes from a lack of concentration.'

The young man was hanging on to the old man's every word. And, not wanting to miss a single one, he didn't dare interrupt him.

'Thanks to concentration,' proceeded the millionaire, 'you will understand why you've been placed in the exact spot where you are in the world. This will appear clearer and clearer to you, and more and more simple. Your mind will be penetrated by a very calming, reassuring thought, making you exclaim as if waking up after a long, deep sleep: "Ah! That's who I am. That's why I'm here at this moment. That's why I'm doing what I'm doing. That's why I'm here with such and such a person." You'll experience what could be called a feeling of destiny. You'll understand your destiny. And a feeling of acceptance will seep into your mind. That doesn't mean that you must resign yourself to your fate. But since you will see with clear-sighted vision the position you're in at that moment, you'll accept it to a certain extent - you will recognise your personal starting point which will help you to guide your future career and to take the reigns of your destiny firmly in your hands.'

The millionaire stopped speaking, taking a moment to bend down once again to inhale the perfume of the rose he had smelled a little while before.

'The rose has been a symbol of life since time began. If you gain control over your mind, you'll understand why. The thorns are the road of experience: the trials and tribulations each one of us must undergo to understand the true beauty of existence.'

Having said this, he pulled a pair of pruning shears out of a pocket, snipped a rose and offered it to his young companion.

'Keep this rose all your life,' he said. 'It will act as a talisman, bringing you good luck. Lady Luck really exists, even though few people know about her. Believe in her. Caress her with your thoughts. Ask her what you want. She will respond. All successful people believe in luck, despite the fact that they are considered superstitious by many. But they're right, you know.

'With this simple rose, know that you are an initiate. You belong to the Order of the Rose. Each time you feel the need, find this rose again. It will give you strength. And each time you have doubts about yourself, each time life seems too difficult to bear, come back to this symbolic rose and remember what it represents. Each ordeal, each problem, each mistake will one day be transformed into a magnificent petal. Like this stem full of thorns, suffering leads to light and will make you attain beauty. Each day, set aside some time to concentrate on the heart of the rose. If there's no rose at hand, take any flower or concentrate on a black dot or shiny object. You can also repeat calmly to yourself the formula that my mentor bequeathed to me: BE STILL THEN, AND KNOW THAT I AM GOD. Stare at the rose or the black dot for longer and longer periods of time. When you are able to do it for twenty minutes, your concentration will be excellent. If your heart becomes like this rose, your life will be transformed.'

The young man barely had time to breathe in the delicate scent of the rose when the old man added: 'Let me repeat what I have said. The secret lies in mental concentration. When your mind has become strong and self-assured through concentration exercises you will come to realise that life's problems no longer have any hold over you. You will then understand what I'm about to say, which might appear self-evident and rather banal. Things are only as important as the mind believes them to be. A problem is a problem only if you think it is.

'What does this mean?' he continued. 'If you consider that nothing is serious, that nothing is truly important, then nothing *will* be serious in your eyes, nothing *will* be truly important. Problems will appear large and overwhelming to you in direct proportion to the weaknesses of your mind. The stronger your mind is, the more insignificant your problems will appear. Such is the secret of eternal peace. So *concentrate*. This is one of the greatest keys to success.

'In fact, all of life is basically a long concentration exercise. The soul is immortal. Passing from life to life, the mind slowly discovers itself and develops. This apprenticeship is generally a long one. And people meet with no more than mitigated success because only those with high levels of concentration manage to reach their goals. Of course, not all successful people have made it a point to practise concentration exercises. But during their successive lives on earth, they achieved a level of concentration that allowed them to succeed more easily than the others. When your mind reaches its highest level of concentration, you will enter that singular state where dreams and reality literally coincide.'

The millionaire and the young man then walked back into the house. The sky had all of a sudden become dark and cloudy; yet early that morning the sun had been radiant. A storm was in the offing, and the house was now so gloomy that the lights had to be turned on. Apparently just for the romantic effect, which the young man was unwilling to say anything against, the old man lit a candelabra with seven candles. He then stood beside the window, where the curtain was blowing in the wind. He pulled it back and glanced up towards the sky. Then he addressed these words to the young man:

'Always remember that at a certain height there are never any clouds. If the clouds in your life are blocking the light, it's because your soul hasn't soared high enough. Most people make the mistake of fighting problems. It's as if they were constantly bent on trying to eliminate the clouds, to dissolve them by some kind of magical process. Of course, they might manage to dissolve them temporarily, but the clouds will always come back to stand between them and the sun, blocking the light, however bright it may be. What you must do is raise yourself above the clouds once and for all. Look at the heart of the rose for longer and longer periods. There you'll find the path that will lead you above the clouds where the sky is forever blue. Don't waste your time chasing the clouds, which unceasingly renew themselves....

'You might not understand everything I've told you now,' he ended, 'but accept it in good faith.'

The millionaire and the young man sat down at the dinner table. The butler arrived, bringing bread and wine, and served them.

'I've been wondering about something for a while,' said the young man. Truthfully, the question had been haunting him since the day before. 'I really do think everything you've been saying is right. And I now believe that if I apply the formula you've given me, I can become a millionaire quickly and attain peace of mind. The only problem is that I'm wondering about the field in which I'll be able to make a fortune.'

The millionaire started to smile. This utterly serious question apparently amused him. 'You must put your trust in life and in the power of your mind,' he said. 'Don't worry. First set your goal, then ask your deep unconscious to steer you towards the path that will lead you to riches. Start by asking; then wait. The answer won't be long in coming.'

The young man appeared sceptical, if not disappointed, with the millionaire's answer. He would no doubt have liked something a little more specific.

The millionaire, obviously a secret mind-reader, winced in sympathy and quickly added: 'You must first find work satisfying to your heart. Then think about it. All the elements of the occupation that could please you are already within you. You simply don't realise it because you aren't yet in tune with your true nature. By concentrating hard, this will happen more and more, and the answers won't stop gushing out. Better still, you will discover what most people desperately seek all of their lives and never find, giving them the feeling that life is absurd. You will uncover the mysterious purpose of your existence on earth. You will understand this not only with your head but with your heart as well. Don't you see that you have everything to gain from concentrating on the heart of the rose? There you will find the be-all and end-all of your existence. With time, you will realise this.'

He stopped for a moment and took a tiny sip of wine. He didn't seem to be drinking, just delicately savouring it. His eyes were closed in a kind of religious reverence.

'But where will I get the money to start?' asked the young man. 'I haven't got a bean.'

'How much will you need?'

'I don't know - at least £10,000. That's how much *you* needed to start.'

'You should be able to find it. Look a little. In your opinion, what avenues are open to you?'

'Truthfully, I can't see any. I don't know of any bank that will back me with a loan. I have no collateral. I have little left over from my salary at the end of the month, and I don't own anything - not even a car....'

'But have you at least tried?'

'No...but I'm positive that....'

'That's a mistake you should never repeat. Don't be like most people, who give up before they even try. That's the best way of never doing anything and never succeeding at anything. Don't fall into the same trap as those who take action but who are inwardly convinced that they won't succeed. They start out as losers. Bring your thoughts and actions into harmony. Be in harmony with yourself.'

'I'm willing all right, but my problem still hasn't been settled. I can always try....'

'You must start out firmly convinced that the solution exists - the ideal solution to your problem. The power of your mind and the magic of your objective will unswervingly attract the solution to you in ways that you probably don't even suspect exist. Be inwardly convinced that you will succeed, and you will. Don't leave room for doubt. Banish it with all the strength your mind can muster. Doubt is part and parcel of the powers of darkness, whereas the optimism you feel belongs to the kingdom of light and life. These two powers are in constant conflict. Struggle staunchly against doubt. For doubt is also a thought, and, like all thoughts, it tends to materialise in your life. If you are firmly convinced that you will get your loan, you will.... Are you convinced that you can get one?'

'Yes. Now I am. You've convinced me.'

'In your present circumstances, what would you do to reach your goal - that is, to get a loan?'

'I don't really know.'

'If you only had a short time - let's say an hour - to get £10,000 to set up your own business, what would you do?'

'I still have no idea....'

'Standing before you is a millionaire who has just encouraged you, given you the secrets of his success, and you don't know what to do? Not one thing comes to mind to get this money?'

It suddenly dawned on the young man what the millionaire was talking about. Perhaps all he needed to do was ask him for the money. After hesitating for a while, that's what he resolved to do.

'Would you lend me the £10,000 I need?'

'There you go. Now, wasn't that easy? All you had to do was ask. But people never dare to ask. *You have to dare to ask.*'

He then pulled out the £10,000 he had been carrying around with him since the young man arrived and which he apparently kept on him as pocket money - an astoundingly large amount in the eyes of most common mortals, but insignificant to him. In any event, it served no purpose since he lived cut off from the outside world.

After casting a nostalgic glance at the wad of money in his hands - a glance which could not be attributed to his giving it away - the millionaire handed it over to the young man. He accepted it, tremulous with emotion. He had never held such a vast sum of money in his life.

'You probably think this money was easy to get,' said the old man. 'But hear me out when I say that there's absolutely no reason why obtaining money in the future will be any more difficult for you. Unfortunately, it is commonly believed that money is hard to come by and that you have to work hard to get it. In fact, the only value of work is to strengthen the fibre of your mind and to force you to think more. When you have earned a lot of money - and I assure you it won't be long in coming if you apply the secrets I've taught you - you will realise that what counts is your mental attitude, the power of your desire and the fact of having been able to channel it by means of a specific monetary objective. Most people fail because they neglect to do this. That's why they are forced to do hard or unappealing work to earn their living. Don't forget that outside circumstances always end up reflecting the state of your mind and the nature of your innermost convictions.'

Overcome with joy at finally owning £10,000, the young man listened to the millionaire's wise words of advice with only half an ear.

'So, remember, young man, when you need money: if you are positive that you can get it easily and quickly, you will. And as soon as doubt begins to invade your mind, think back to the £10,000 you've just obtained. All you need to do is ask. If you are convinced that you will get what you ask for at the very moment you ask, if you pretend that you have it already, then you will get it. Remember, our deepest convictions always come true.'

'What if I start to have doubts?'

'When you do, the best way to get rid of them is to apply some self-suggestion and repeat opposite thoughts. Turn your words into royal decrees. When your mind has become powerful enough, each one of them will become a kind of command. Your words and reality will become one. And the time it takes for your commands to be accomplished will become briefer and briefer, and finally instantaneous. By then, you will have learned truly to master yourself. You must become the master of your thoughts so as to avoid having thoughts that could harm others. You must acquire the ability to think only positive thoughts for the good of others, so that the power of your words doesn't turn against you.'

He again took a slight pause.

'This money...,' he went on, pointing to the wad of banknotes, 'well, I'm not lending it to you....'

He seemed to hesitate a second, no doubt skilfully planning a bigger effect, a ploy which in fact did the trick, judging by the young man's reaction.

'I'm not lending it to you... I'm giving it to you,' said the millionaire. 'By doing so, everything will have turned full circle. This money is pure and clean. It was given to me by my mentor to start me out in business. Don't use it for any other reason. Don't imitate the man in the Bible who buried his coins instead of letting them work for him. So many people act that way. They are making the worst mistake ever. They're letting fear be their guide. Fear is your worst enemy, the brother of doubt, and you must conquer it. Be fearless and bold. Anyone who, under the pretext of rationality, buries the money he has received is not worthy of it. He doesn't deserve more, and it's highly unlikely that he will get more. He is disobeying one of the greatest laws of life, the law of abundance. Money must flow freely to be able to multiply.'

The young man was savouring his money just as much as his generous benefactor's words.

'The money I'm giving you is, however, at heart a loan,' the millionaire continued. 'One day you, in turn, must give it to someone else. Many years from now you will meet a young man in the same situation as you are in now. You'll recognise him by a sign - he'll be wearing a rose. You must give him the money I'm giving you today. Make sure that by then it represents an insignificant amount to you: pocket money and no more. I bid you to do as I have done - you must give him the equivalent of what this amount represents today. Then he, too, may start out with a substantial amount, because if inflation keeps up at the rate it's going, £10,000 won't be worth much by then.'

The young man nodded his head in agreement.

'When accepting this money, the next young man must also solemnly swear to convey the lessons that I have taught you and that you will hand down to him. Don't break this chain under any pretext, otherwise, it will bring you bad luck. I know you're an honest fellow: that's why I'm not afraid to bequeath this secret to you.'

Full of gratitude, the young man thanked him warmly.

'There's one more important thing you must know....'

Just then, the storm broke out. The millionaire stopped for a minute and his face wore a sombre expression. It began to rain. 'All the signs are coming to pass,' he muttered to himself. 'As I said,' he addressed the young man again, 'there's one more thing you need to know: the supreme secret I have handed down to you is valid for reaching all of the goals you will set for yourself. Truthfully, the reason I amassed such a colossal fortune is not that money interested me so much. It was basically only a way to show men of little faith the power of the mind.'

He paused briefly again, but the young man didn't dare ask him a question. Then he continued: 'Man's greatest possession is freedom. Wealth gives freedom. And it'll be good for you to know this freedom. With it, you will see many an illusion vanish. You'll also understand that true freedom is found in detachment, which is the highest form of freedom. Only he who leaves with empty hands will be able to tend the eternal roses. Achieving this freedom was the secret goal of my entire existence. Despite what others thought - people who judge only by appearances and saw me only as a prosperous businessman - I have never been anything other than a humble gardener.'

The young man then asked him: 'Why have you told me all these things? Why have you given me this money? You didn't owe *me* anything.... In fact, it could have been somebody else who came to see you....'

'But that's just it. No one else did come. Your desire led you to me. This is what happens in all of life's circumstances. Hasn't it been said that, once the disciple is ready, the master appears? Besides, I've received a lot. It's normal for me to give.'

'Maybe,' said the young man, unwilling to back down. 'But why me rather than somebody else?'

The Instant Millionaire smiled. 'You're stubborn. I like that.' Then he lost his stern and distant look for the very first time and gave the young man a warm, fatherly look. 'If you want to know the real reason, I'll tell you. I don't know if you're capable of accepting it today. But one day perhaps you will.... The soul is eternal. And each soul travels from one life to another surrounded by companions. Each companion helps the other to fulfil his destiny. The encounters we have during our lifetime are never the result of coincidence. And it's rare to meet someone for the very first time. You were my father in a previous life. Isn't it right for you to be my spiritual son in this life?'

The young man was overwhelmed with emotion, even though he wasn't sure that he really understood what he was hearing. The millionaire approached him. Never before had the young man found him so regal in bearing. Despite his old age he walked like a king, tall and straight. His glowing face looked untouched by the years. With his right index finger the millionaire lightly touched the young man on the forehead, saying: 'Discover who you really are. The truth will forever set you free.'

Those were the last words the millionaire uttered. Outside, the storm had abated as quickly as it had begun and the sun was shining brightly again. The light shed by the candelabra was no longer needed. The millionaire picked it up and carried it away with him without uttering a word. The young man did not dare say anything. He found himself alone, his head teeming with thoughts, his hands holding the money the old man had given him.

CHAPTER 15

In which the young man and the old man embark on different journeys

THE young man did not remain alone for long. Suddenly the butler reappeared, holding an envelope. He handed it to the young man, explaining: 'My master entrusted me with the task of giving this to you. He insisted that you should read it in the privacy of your room. You can spend another day here. Then you must go. These are my master's wishes.'

The young man thanked him and, dying with curiosity to discover the contents of the document, obediently retired to his room. This time, however, he took the precaution of leaving the door slightly ajar for fear of being locked in again.

He sat on the edge of the bed, hastily tore the envelope open and pulled out a letter. It was beautifully handwritten in black ink and a delicate scent of roses wafted from it.

'These are my last requests,' it read. 'I am leaving you all the books in my library. They will come in very handy to you. Do not make the same mistake most people make with books. Some believe that the contents of books are utterly worthless. They believe that they themselves are reinventing the world. And since they have not benefited from the knowledge found in books, they unfortunately repeat the mistakes made by their forefathers. In this way, they waste a lot of time and a lot of money.

'Don't fall into the other trap, either: trusting implicitly in what books contain and letting those who came before you do your thinking for you. Worthy people for the most part, the authors of these books have travelled for many years and seen many things. A book is always, to some extent, the retelling of a voyage. But the journey you will undertake is not identical to theirs. Retain only what outlasts the passage of time. As for the rest, use your most precious asset: your head. It's still the best invention when it comes to thinking, so I hear. Unfortunately, most people spend their lives looking for ways to avoid thinking. Such is human nature: the inclination for an easy way out, in appearance at least. Nature and instinct conquer most people. Make sure that your mind is victorious.

'Since our first encounter, I have tried to convey to you the pearls of wisdom I have been able to glean during my long life. In this document you will find a few thoughts that represent my spiritual legacy. I would like you to do your best to communicate them to as many people as you can. As such, my life will be justified. Tell people about our encounter and the secret you have learned. Before doing so, however, you must try it out. A method that has not been tried and tested is completely worthless. Within six years you will be a millionaire. At that time you will be free to undertake the necessary steps to transmit my legacy to people and talk about our meeting.

'Now I must leave you. My roses have already been kept waiting for too long.'

Despite being choked with emotion, the young man felt in the envelope again and found the Instant Millionaire's will. It was in its own large envelope, closed with a big red wax seal in the shape of a rose. The young man carefully broke open the seal and took out the document, which was several pages long.

This extraordinary testament was handwritten in ample, majestic letters which seemed to breathe as if imbued with their own life. The young man became engrossed in the will for a whole hour, which seemed no more than a few minutes.

When he had finished reading, he naturally wanted to go and thank the millionaire for having given him such a precious gift. He went quickly back to the dining room. There was nobody there. He called out to the butler. No answer. Since the sun was shining again after the storm he thought the millionaire must have returned to his roses. He was right, but the old man had gone back to join them for a very different reason.

The young man ran out to the garden and called the millionaire. Suddenly, he spotted him. Strangely enough, the old man was lying right in the middle of a path, at the foot of a rose bush. Near him lay the candelabra: only one candle was still burning, the tallest one - all the others had gone out. At first the young man thought the millionaire was merely sleeping, taking a catnap in an unusual place - he was, after all, quite eccentric. But the nearer he drew the more troubled he became, as if sensing that something very serious were happening.

When he finally reached the millionaire's side, his fears were confirmed. The old man had put on a white robe that reached to his ankles. His hands, folded upon his chest, held a single rose. His face betrayed no anguish, no trace of suffering. It was perfectly serene: he was dead, just as the young man had suspected. He confirmed this by kneeling down and placing his ear over the old man's mouth. He was no longer breathing, even though his entire being exuded supernatural happiness.

'What a strange way to die!' exclaimed the young man to himself. The millionaire had known the exact moment he was going to leave. Who knows if he had not ordered the precise moment of his departure by some strange, secret means known only to him, or simply by implacably willing himself to die? The young man would never know. The millionaire had taken his secret with him.

The young man then sensed that it was time for him, too, to leave. There was nothing more to do here. Just before going, however, he thought he could perhaps take the millionaire's rose with him as a souvenir. He bent down over the inert body and stretched out his hand. He touched the rose, but suddenly pulled his hand away, deciding not to take it. He felt that by doing so he would desecrate the millionaire's memory. That rose belonged to him. It was his final companion. The young man stood up, catching a glimpse of the candelabra with the central candle still strangely burning. Tears filled his eyes. He had not known the millionaire for long, and yet he had become deeply attached to him as if he had been his father.

He solemnly vowed then and there never to betray the millionaire. He would convey his teachings as best he could. At the very instant he pronounced this solemn oath, the last candle blew out.

The young man left the same way he had arrived, tightly clutching the millionaire's last will and testament against his chest.

The next day, the millionaire's library was delivered to his house. It was so immense that it left little room for the rest of his things. In fact, the young man was immediately confronted with a dilemma: either to move out or to get rid of some of the books. He chose to move out. And he did it with a light heart. Wasn't this a sign of a new life ahead of him?

EPILOGUE

JUST as the millionaire had predicted, the young man made his first million before his six-year deadline was up. He therefore kept his promise. He took a month off to write down his encounter with the Instant Millionaire and the philosophy that he had taught him.

THE INSTANT MILLIONAIRE

Further copies of this book are available at your local bookshop or newsagent, or they can be ordered by sending a copy of this form to:

Hammond Direct
20 Rowan Road
Bexleyheath
Kent   DA7 4BW

Please include the following amount to cover postage and packing:

	First book	Each additional book
U.K. (including BFPO)	£1	40p
Europe (including Eire)	£1.50	70p
Rest of World	£2.50	£1.50

NAME AND ADDRESS IN BLOCK LETTERS PLEASE

NAME ....

ADDRESS ....

....

....

....

....

Number of copies required ....   Total cost @ £4.99 each   £............

Postage and Packing   £............

Total amount enclosed   £............

Please send a cheque, postal order or international money order, payable to HAMMOND DIRECT.

Prices are correct at time of going to press. While every effort is made to keep prices low, it is sometimes necessary to increase prices at short notice. Hammond reserve the right to charge new retail prices which may differ from those advertised.

90100